Special Report 15

A study of the economic impact of the Invergordon Aluminium Smelter

G A Mackay

A Highlands and Islands Development Board Publication

ρ3⁸⁸

SBN 902347 61 6

Contents

	Page
Acknowledgements	4
CHAPTER 1: Problems and policies in the Highlands	5
CHAPTER 2: The East Ross economy	12
CHAPTER 3: The advent of British Aluminium	17
CHAPTER 4: Growth centre policies	30
CHAPTER 5: The input-output model	37
CHAPTER 6: The construction phase	44
CHAPTER 7: The permanent phase	53
CHAPTER 8: Labour market impact	61
CHAPTER 9: Summary and conclusions	79
Bibliography	88

Acknowledgements

This report emanates from a wider study of the social and economic impact of the Invergordon aluminium smelter on the local community and economy. In 1969 the Highlands and Islands Development Board (HIDB) and The British Aluminium Co. Ltd. (BA) commissioned a two-year study from the University of Aberdeen and I was appointed as the research fellow in the Department of Political Economy. In 1971 the University obtained a further two-year grant from the Social Science Research Council, primarily to allow the investigation to look at the more permanent effects of the smelter's operations. The study was completed in 1974 but certain problems, other work and the need for some updating in the light of the oil-related developments which subsequently occurred in the Invergordon area have delayed the publication of the final report.

In the first place, therefore, thanks must be given to the HIDB, BA and SSRC, not only for financing the study but also for the interest and enthusiasm they have expressed throughout the course of the work. Much of this interest was channelled through an informal steering group set up in the early days of the study, with representatives from the sponsors, the university, Ross and Cromarty County Council and other interested parties. This steering group provided a tremendous amount of help and encouragement. Of those participating in the group I would like particularly to express my sincere thanks to Donald John MacKay, Gordon Drummond and Pat Bowman of British Aluminium; Frank Spaven, Gordon Adams, Alasdair Munro, Stan Pickett and Bob Storey of the HIDB; Chris Harley and George Pease of the old Ross and Cromarty County Council; and Douglas Calder of the old Inverness County Council.

Their organizations provided a great deal of help and through them I would like to thank the many colleagues who were involved. Much of the data required for the study was collected by way of questionnaires and other surveys and it is therefore essential to put on record my gratitude to the many individuals, firms and other bodies who kindly devoted time to providing the information required for a study of this type.

Colleagues in Aberdeen University have been a frequent source of ideas and inspiration and I would like to express my lifelong thanks to my supervisor, Max Gaskin, and Donald MacKay of the Department of Political Economy; to Adrian Varwell, my counterpart on the social study, and Mick Carter of the Department of Sociology; and to John Smith of the Department of Geography.

Finally, I would like to thank the secretarial staff of the Department of Political Economy, particularly Willa Fraser who has endured my obscure handwriting and other problems for many years.

I should add the usual note that the views expressed in this thesis are my own and do not necessarily reflect those of any other individual or body; but I hope that it will be clear to the reader that without the help of those mentioned above, I would never have been in a position to formulate those views.

Tony Mackay

1 Problems and policies in the Highlands

Regional problems and policies have attracted increasing attention in recent years. This is a consequence of the acceptance of the power and responsibility of governments to control the level of economic activity. As economic activity by its very nature cannot be uniformly dispersed throughout the various regions of an economy, it is to be expected that different regions will have markedly different economic structures and performances. Klaassen has identified four types of region[1]: the prosperous region, in which both the level and rate of growth of economic activity are high; the potentially depressed region, in which the level of activity is still high but the expected growth rate low; the developing distressed region, in which the expected rate of growth is high but the present level of activity low; and the depressed region, in which both the level and the expected rate of growth of economic activity are low. Clearly this classification could be refined but it provides a useful start.

The present concern is with a special case of the depressed region: the sparsely populated (or marginal) region, frequently remote from the main centres of population. Within Western Europe a number of regions fall into this category — the southern part of Italy, northern Scandinavia, the south and west of France, most of the Irish Republic — and in the United Kingdom the striking examples are parts of Wales and the Highlands and Islands of Scotland.

Although it is difficult to generalize about such regions, certain common characteristics can usually be identified. Depopulation, low levels of income, comparatively high levels of unemployment, low activity rates and a large primary economic sector are often observable. From a consideration of the fundamental economic changes that have taken place in most Western economies in recent centuries, it will be seen that employment in the primary (resource) industries has declined substantially with parallel increases in the numbers employed in secondary (manufacturing) and tertiary (service) industries. Most sparsely populated regions are still heavily dependent on the primary sector, particularly agriculture and "the evidence presented . . . clearly shows that, with the exception of certain industrial areas characterized by a predominance of stagnating or declining sectors, the regions in greatest economic difficulty are those which are the most agricultural. Moreover, the difficulties experienced by agricultural regions are qualitatively different, since for the most part the essential problem is one of stimulating the initial growth of a modern economy, rather than of converting an already industrial region from one type of activity to another."[2]

These characteristics, particularly the continuing importance of the primary sector, have led to comparisons with the 'dual economy' syndrome in many of the underdeveloped countries of the world and to assertions that the problems of sparsely populated areas are derived from the fact that they

---

[1]. L.H. Klaassen: *Area economic and social redevelopment* (Paris, 1965), pp. 28-30.

[2] N.M. Hansen: *French regional planning* (Bloomington, 1968)

have been bypassed by the various revolutions in agriculture, industry and technology. Although such comparisons can provide useful insights, the general hypothesis is incorrect: what has usually happened is that certain local factors were so strong as to affect these revolutions in such ways that their effects have been very different from their effects on most regions of Western Europe and North America.

Some of these factors may in fact be common to various regions while others will be peculiar to one particular region. Some generalization is possible, e.g. with regard to physical structure, distance from the main markets for agricultural and manufactured produce, the distribution of population with ensuing consequences for the provision of public services and retail distribution etc. It should be stressed, nevertheless, that there frequently exist local factors which invalidate the implications of such generalizations and which require detailed consideration in the formulation of policies for solving the problems.

One further point must be made by way of introduction. This is that the identification of a problem and, presumably, the choice of an appropriate set of policy measures depend on the objectives of the individual or body concerned. In any situation there are likely to be conflicting objectives. In the Highlands and Islands it is frequently asserted that the objectives of those concerned with the evolution and execution of policies to develop the region are in conflict with the objectives of local inhabitants. The situation is further confused because within the local population there are distinct groups with differing interests and objectives. Almost inevitably, therefore, there is disagreement about the nature of problems and the policies required to solve such problems.

The definition used here for the Highlands and Islands[3] is the now common one of the seven crofting counties of Argyll, Caithness, Inverness, Orkney, Ross and Cromarty, Sutherland and Zetland. This is an area of some 14,500 square miles and a population of only 285,000, giving an average density of less than twenty people to the square mile (compared with 95 in other rural areas of the United Kingdom and 910 in Central Scotland). The area stretches for over four hundred miles from the northern isles of Shetland to the Mull of Kintyre. This is about one fifth of the total land mass of the United Kingdom, covering a large number of inhabited islands — and inhabited mainland peninsulas more inaccessible than islands — and for the provision of education, transport and public services in general, the sheer physical extent of inhabited country presents a difference of degree so great as to constitute a difference of kind. One fifth of the population lives on crofts[4] and a further two fifths in settlements of less than 1,000 people.

The region is not really homogeneous on economic, cultural, historical or other criteria and evolved mainly for administrative purposes. It is useful sometimes to regard the Highlands as three distinct areal economies. The first (and most prosperous) is the fairly urbanized area around the Beauly and Cromarty Firths, which extends in a narrowing belt of

---

[3] Hereafter, "the Highlands" is frequently used as a synonym for the Highlands and Islands.

[4] A crofter is a part-time smallholder with special rights including hereditary security of tenure of an individual piece of land with a share in the common grazing rights of his township.

orthodox lowland-type farming up the east coast and reappears in Caithness and in the Orkney Isles. This area has recently experienced an influx of large-scale manufacturing industry. The second distinct area is the eastern and southern Highlands, an upland farming area very popular with tourists in that it is close to Glasgow and Central Scotland. Finally, there is the western and northern periphery, including the Hebrides and the Orkney and Shetland Isles, in which the staple activities are crofting and fishing. Alternatively, three distinct cultural areas can be distinguished: the lowland area around the Beauly and Cromarty Firths; the north-east and northern isles with their Norse and Viking ancestries; and the traditionally Gaelic communities of the West Coast and Western Isles. Obviously, generalizations are difficult and even the above categorization may be misleading.

Usually, however, the "Highland problem" is expressed in terms of a declining population and an ageing population structure. The 1971 Census of Scotland does in fact show a slight increase in population for the region, but before 1971 the population had been declining for over a century and there always has been a high level of emigration. Even though the 1971 figures disguise a continuing high level of net emigration which is offset by natural increase, it appears to be the case that the Highland economy is experiencing an upturn, the reasons for which are discussed below.

The population of the Highlands has declined substantially over the last century. It was at its highest in the middle of the nineteenth century: in 1831, the census recorded a population of nearly 390,000. It was highest in Argyll in 1831; in Inverness-shire in 1841; in Ross and Cromarty and Sutherland in1851, and in Caithness, Orkney and Zetland in 1861. If we take the 1971 populations as percentages of the highest figures for each county, the respective percentages are: Inverness 92.0; Ross and Cromarty 70.6; Caithness 69.8; Argyll 59.4; Zetland 55.5; Orkney 53.3; Sutherland 50.9. These figures are depressing but they are even more so given that the present-day age structure of the population is heavily weighted towards the older end of the scale and has very few people in the 15-45 age group.

Nevertheless, although the general picture has been one of decline, certain areas have shown significant increases and, indeed, the slight increase in population shown by the 1971 figures is attributable to these areas,, mainly concentrated along what may be called the central axis of the Highland mainland from Cowal and mid-Argyll in the south-west, through Lochaber and the Great Glen north eastwards to Inverness, East Ross and Caithness. It is in this relatively accessible zone that services have become concentrated and the striking examples of industrial growth have occurred. In the context of Highland development three areas are often put forward as major growth centres — Lochaber, the Moray Firth and Caithness. The growth of these centres has raised interesting problems for policy, particularly regarding settlement distribution since there has also been a steady movement away from the rural or 'landward' areas (as they are known) into the towns of the region. In 1931, for example, 34.7% of the population lived in the landward parts of the region, but this fell to 29.6% by 1961 and to 26.4% by 1971.

The presentation of the Highland problem in demographic terms, however, is essentially regarding it from a symptomatic point of view rather than a causal one, although the trends of decline and landward-town movement of themselves create problems, particularly for the provision of infrastructure and public services and for the availability of labour. Underlying these population trends is the decline of employment in the primary sector and the difficulty of providing alternative employment opportunities. If this decline is not counteracted by positive developments in other sectors of the economy, unemployment and emigration almost inevitably in time induce a self-generating process of decay.

The relationship between employment opportunities, in terms of both quality and quantity, and emigration is crucial in the case of young people. Probably the most disturbing feature of the region's recent social and economic life has been the steady emigration of young people, particularly those with skills and further educational qualifications. It has been asserted that migration is primarily a consequence of the failure to fulfil certain basic aspirations in the home community[5] and it appears that in the Highlands such dissatisfaction is concerned with employment opportunities, future prospects and the standard of leisure facilities and social activities. This problem is considered in greater detail below.

At this stage it is necessary to introduce the rather simplistic theory of regional economic growth known as the export-base theory. Although in its more refined forms the theory demonstrates certain fundamental inadequacies, its general propositions are of relevance in the present context. The export-base theory divides total employment in a regional economy into two sectors — the basic sector and the service sector. The basic sector is defined as those industries earning income from outside the region,[6] i.e. by exporting (and this would include primary and manufactured products and receipts from tourism, for example). It is this export (or basic) income which allows the economy to sustain its particular level of services[7] — education, transport, retail trade etc. — and the service sector can therefore be seen as being dependent on the total level of population or employment in the economy and consequently on the level of employment in the basic sector. Surveys suggest that in a stable economy the basic and service sectors will be of roughly equal size (i.e. a 1:1 ratio).[8] If the basic sector expands, so will the service sector and total population and employment; and the converse. The source of growth (or decline) in a regional economy is therefore the exporting sector and policies for development must have export earnings as their basic objective.

The peculiar employment structure which still persists in the Highlands can be seen from Table 1.1 which also sets out comparable figures for Scotland and the United Kingdom. The data relates to employees as at June 1968.

---

[5] S.N. Eisenstadt: *The absorption of emigrants* (London, 1954)

[6] Over and above the local subsistance element in any economy.

[7] In a regional context, grants from central government funds can be regarded as income from outside the region.

[8] See, for example, A.J. Brown: *The Framework of Regional Economics in the United Kingdom* (Cambridge, 1972), chapter 8.

Table 1.1

Percentage distribution of employment

	Highlands	Scotland	United Kingdom
Primary industries	10.7%	5.4%	3.9%
Manufacturing	11.7%	34.9%	38.0%
Construction	14.4%	8.9%	6.7%
Services	63.3%	50.8%	51.1%

Source: Department of Employment

In that the data excludes the self-employed, who in certain sectors (e.g. agriculture and fishing) are numerically important, the figures are not precisely representative of the region's employment structure. The primary sector is comprised of the agriculture, fishing and forestry industries together with a small amount of mining. The figure of 10.7% underestimates the numerical importance of this sector in that it does not necessarily include crofters, who may be included under other headings according to their supplementary employments. There are presently about 15,500 working units (as distinct from crofts) in the Highlands. Nevertheless, the relative importance of the primary sector and the minor role of the manufacturing (secondary) sector are obvious from Table 1.1. The high figure for the service sector is attributable mainly to tourist-related activities and to assistance from central government funds for infrastructure, transport undertakings etc. Including employment in the tourist industry together with primary and secondary exporting industries in the Highlands would give a basic: service ratio of approximately 1:2 and it is this inevitable instability (a consequence of long-run decline and over-capacity in the service sector) which is at the root of many economic (and non-economic) problems in the Highlands.

Before specifically considering the prospects for expansion of the basic sector of the economy, however, it is necessary to return to the point made earlier about the importance of peculiar local factors. A cursory examination of the economic history of the Highlands would show that there have previously been periods during which the basic sector was both relatively large and prosperous: the best examples concern the kelp and fishing industries in the late eighteenth and early nineteenth centuries. The export earnings accruing to these industries unfortunately did little to stimulate the growth of the economy and on their eventual decline the familiar processes continued.

The main reason for this failure was the lack of the entrepreneurial middle class which played an important role in the agricultural, industrial and technological revolutions elsewhere. This was a consequence of the system of landholding which had evolved from the old clan days. "The wealth of the Highlands, produced by the small peasantry that occupied most of the land, was divided on lines determined by the old hierarchy of the clans between landlords, tacksmen and peasants. Individuality in the purely economic field could scarcely break through this rigid framework with its guaranteed incomes and positions."[9] Export earnings accrued

---

[9] M. Gray: *The Highland economy, 1750-1850* (Edinburgh, 1957) p.13

almost wholly to the small group of landlords, most of whom were heavily indebted to others outwith the Highlands and little interested in using this income within the region.

When development opportunities arose in the fishing and kelp industries, there was insufficient local capital and entrepreneurship to take advantage and the expansion of the exporting sector was mainly the achievement of outsiders. A similar situation arose when sheep farming spread throughout the region in the early decades of the nineteenth century: those who profited had "ready money as well as commercial sense and technical expertise. Traditional society, in all its grades, was short in all those requirements. A few tacksmen, perhaps, might have the capital, but their attitude to the farming they knew did not promise the ready experimental outlook and the ruthless commercial adaptability demanded by fresh enterprise."[10]

Thus the pattern of landholding and agricultural production exerted a strong pressure on potential entrepreneurs to do nothing or to leave the Highlands and where opportunities arose only outsiders were capable of taking them. Furthermore, the strong Calvinist traditions of many Highlanders were opposed to particular types of development. The result was that much of the income created in the region immediately flowed out . . . and this is a problem that still holds. Today, much of the capital invested in the Highlands is owned by people or institutions outwith the Highlands. Opportunities for local entrepreneurship are limited and absentee landholding is extensive.

The importance of these factors in the historical development of the Highlands has been recognised by many commentators but the wrong conclusion has frequently been reached: namely, that to attempt to strengthen the links with the more developed economy of the rest of the United Kingdom would prove even more harmful. In contrast, rather, the development of the Highlands must depend on the basic (exporting) industries. Although their performance in the past has been disappointing (harmful, in cases), the task is not to seek radical alternatives but to ensure that a greater proportion of the export earnings of the basic industries remains in the Highlands and is used for the diversification and stabilization of the economy.

The Highland and Islands have a long history of official and unofficial agencies concerned with the development of the region. The permanency of many of the problems can be seen from the lack of success of the policies which have been pursued. Patrick Sellar and William Young (whose attempts at developing the Highlands earned them notoriety) wrote to the Countess of Sutherland in 1809 in these terms:

"The Country in its time may not produce gold or silver or wine or oil, but (they assured the Countess) if it produce industry all these things will be added unto it. If your Ladyship can lead the people from destroying the Soil, and from starving every creature on it, to settle in villages; if you can introduce a few Mechanics and manufacturers among them; induce the farmers to the cultivation of flax; set a woollen manufacture such as we have at Elgin ageing; and get the sons and daughters of the present generation into the employment of those who can teach them industry and

---

[10] Ibid, p. 91

10

which considering the pliability, and the acuteness too, of the people, seems no very Herculean undertaking, the present enchantment which keeps them down will be broken, and Sutherland may enjoy as many comforts and pay as fair rent as any of her neighbours."[11]

It will be seen, therefore, that policy objectives have changed little over the years. In economic terms the essential aims have been to increase the employment potential of existing industries and to attract new industries to the region. Given fairly unanimous agreement that the Highlands and Islands have a distinct and unique culture, the desire to protect this culture has conditioned attempts at industrial promotion, particularly in respect of the spatial distribution of population and employment. For example, a great deal of effort has been concerned with the development of crofting and fishing and forestry industries, which by their very nature can utilize dispersed labour markets.

---

[11] Quoted in E. Richards: *The leviathan of wealth* (London, 1973), p. 173

2 East Ross economy

The study area for the economic study has been taken as the probable area of impact of the aluminium smelter at Invergordon[1]. At the outset there was the usual problem of defining this area prior to the impact occurring. Various alternatives were tried but all were heavily constrained by the availability of published statistics. A great deal of data at the local level is available only for local authority areas (e.g. burghs and districts of county) and employment data is usually only available for employment office areas. Luckily the area covered by the Dingwall and Invergordon employment offices coincides closely with the normal travel-to-work area and existing local authority boundaries fitted in well. This enabled the assembly and analysis of a large volume of historical data on the East Ross economy and some of this is summarised below.

The area covered by the economic study is known as East Ross (including the Black Isle) and comprises the burghs of Cromarty, Dingwall, Fortrose, Invergordon and Tain, and districts of county of Avoch, Dingwall, Fearn, Fortrose, Invergordon, Nuir-of-Ord and Tain. The population data set out below is for this area. The employment data is for a slightly smaller area but there do not appear to be any fundamental differences between the two sets of data.

The recent population figures are set out in Table 2.1. Since the second world war the rate of population decline has slowed down but between 1951 and 1961 the area still lost people, despite some natural increase. It will be seen from the table that the total population fell by 1.9% between 1951 and 1961, with a 6.1% increase in the burghal population being offset by a 5.0% decline in the districts. This is a fairly common pattern of drift from the landward areas to the towns and the only exception was the small burgh of Cromarty.

It was necessary to obtain base-line data for the study but it is impossible to obtain precise data for years other than Census years. The Registrar General publishes estimates of the population of local authority areas in Scotland each year and the 1968 estimates are set out in Table 2.1. It should be stressed that these are estimates and, particularly for small areas, should be treated with caution as it is difficult to assess accurately changes in migration from year to year. Information from local surveys undertaken by the Development Department of the old Ross and Cromarty County Council suggests that the 1968 estimates were probably slightly too high but they do give nevertheless a reasonable indication of the main trends. Certainly, the population of East Ross increased slightly during the 1960s prior to the establishment of the smelter. Most of this increase occurred in Invergordon and is probably attributable to the opening of the Invergordon whisky distillery. During the period 1961-1968 the population of the burghs increased by 4.3%, with Cromarty again being the only one to show a decline, and that of the districts increased by 0.1% with some of the districts continuing to decline sharply.

---

[1] This is wider than the area used for the social study.

Table 2.1 — Population data, 1951 - 1968

	1951	1961	1968	% change 1951-1961	% change 1961-1968
Small burghs					
Cromarty	726	605	585	-16.7	-3.3
Dingwall	3,436	3,883	3,906	+13.0	+0.6
Fortrose	892	903	996	+1.2	+10.3
Invergordon	1,621	1,686	1,948	+4.0	+15.5
Tain	1,600	1,699	1,716	+6.2	+1.0
Total	8,275	8,776	9,151	+6.1	+4.3
Districts of county					
Avoch	3,102	2,984	3,100	-3.8	+3.9
Dingwall	3,969	3,841	4,100	-3.2	+6.7
Fearn	2,626	2,325	2,200	-11.5	-5.4
Fortrose	1,280	1,181	1,050	-7.7	-11.1
Invergordon	3,343	3,135	2,950	-6.2	-5.9
Muir-of-Ord	4,938	4,938	5,150	+0.0	+4.3
Tain	1,923	1,718	1,600	-10.7	-6.9
Total	21,181	20,122	20,150	-5.0	+0.1
Total	29,456	28,898	29,301	-1.9	+1.4

Sources: Decennial Censuses
1968 Annual Estimates

Another important aspect of the area's population prior to 1968 was the unhealthy age structure with very high proportions of children and retired people. Table 2.2 sets out the percentage figures by age group for East Ross, the Highlands and Islands, Scotland and Great Britain from the 1961 Census.

Table 2.2 — Age structure, 1961

	0-14	15-24	25-34	35-44	45-54	55-64	65+
East Ross	26.9	11.9	11.8	12.4	12.9	10.6	13.5
Highlands and Islands	24.5	11.8	11.8	12.1	13.5	12.1	14.3
Scotland	25.9	13.7	12.7	12.9	13.2	11.0	10.6
Great Britain	23.3	13.2	12.7	13.5	13.9	11.6	11.8

The low proportions in East Ross in the work age groups of 15-64 reflect the high emigration from the area of economically active people and in this respect East Ross is very similar with the Highlands and Islands as a whole. Indeed, the situation has worsened markedly in the younger age groups since 1951: in that year 13% of the population was aged 15-24, 13.4% 25-34 and 14.0% 35-44.

East Ross, including the Black Isle, is one of the best farming areas in Scotland, with good soils and climate. The main activities are the growing of crops (particularly barley, oats and mixed grain, turnips and swedes) and the rearing of sheep and beef cattle.[2] Forestry and fishing are not very important, although salmon fishing provides some employment during the summer months. The main manufacturing activity is whisky distilling, with six distilleries in the area. In 1968, other manufacturing establishments were small and many of them were linked closely with the agricultural sector. During the 1960s there was little change in the structure of manufacturing industry with the only new plans being a large distillery at Invergordon (opened in 1960), an agricultural engineer's and a wool grower's plant. As in many similar areas, the construction sector has been an important but volatile source of activity and employment, as from time to time there have been large individual projects such as hydro-electric works, road schemes — and the aluminium smelter itself, of course. Finally, there is the large service sector, which grew steadily throughout the 1960s, particularly in terms of female employment. Dingwall was the administrative centre for Ross and Cromarty so there is a larger than proportionate number of service jobs in the area and many of the burghs serve as market towns for the agricultural hinterlands.

The detailed employment structure in 1968 is given in Table 2.3, using the Department of Employment's ERII figures, which are subject to the qualifications made earlier. It will be seen that some 15.7% of total employment is in the primary sector, 11.1% in manufacturing, 17.3% in construction and 55.9% in services. This distribution is not much different from that of the Highlands as a whole, as given in Table 1.1 above, but is substantially different from the distribution of employment in Scotland and the U.K. in that East Ross has a very small manufacturing sector. This sector had in fact grown in size since 1960 when it employed only 445 (6.0% of total employment) and obversely the primary sector had contracted from 1,769 employees (24.0%) to the 1968 level of 1,141.

[2] More detailed discussions are given in J. Ormiston: *Moray Firth: An agricultural study* (Inverness, 1973) and North of Scotland College of Agriculture: *An agroeconomic appraisal of agriculture in Easter Ross* (Aberdeen, 1967).

Table 2.3 — Employment structure, 1968

Industry	Males	Females	Total
Agriculture	885	107	992
Forestry	60	3	63
Fishing	53		53
Mining and quarrying	33		33
Food, drink and tobacco	378	47	425
All other manufacturing	332	50	382
Construction	1,186	68	1,254
Gas, electricity and water	244	49	293
Transport and communication	297	77	374
Distributive trades	390	366	756
Insurance, banking etc.	77	60	137
Professional and scientific services	225	744	969
Miscellaneous services	472	619	1,091
Public administration and defence	287	116	403
Industry not stated	31	7	38
Total	4,950	2,313	7,263

Source: Department of Employment

The prime indicator of the area's economic ill health, however, is the unemployment data. The two main features are rates of unemployment, generally higher than those in Scotland (which in turn are usually higher than those for the U.K.) and large seasonal fluctuations.

During the early 1960s the percentage unemployment rates were usually in the band 3% - 7% but from 1965 onwards there was a steady upward trend, reaching a peak of 11% in January 1968. This can be seen even more clearly from a comparison of the local statistics and comparable figures for Scotland. Increasing divergence since late 1964 is clearly evident and since 1968 the unemployment rate in East Ross was frequently twice that of Scotland as a whole. The main causes of the deterioration were the problems facing the Invergordon distillery, which laid off around 200 people in 1966-1967, reducing its labour force to around 160. It should also be noted that most of the unemployed were males although females were not immune to the substantial seasonal fluctuations. In 1968 in East Ross the average monthly unemployment rate was 7.5% equivalent to about 600 people. Table 2.4 sets out the male, female and total percentages and the ratios of the total figures to their Scottish equivalents.

Table 2.4 — Unemployment data, 1968

| | Monthly percentages | | | East Ross as % of Scottish figures |
	Males	Females	Total	
January	13.0	5.9	11.0	256
February	11.1	5.7	9.5	232
March	9.8	4.8	8.3	208
April	9.2	4.5	7.8	200
May	7.9	2.7	6.4	173
June	7.4	2.1	5.9	164
July	5.8	2.8	5.0	162
August	7.3	2.6	5.9	155
September	7.5	2.5	6.0	167
October	8.5	3.3	7.0	194
November	9.2	5.5	8.1	219
December	9.0	6.2	8.2	228

Source: Department of Employment

3 The advent of British Aluminium

The need to attract additional manufacturing employment to East Ross was obvious but this was true of many areas in Scotland and the U.K. In the event, Invergordon was successful and it is interesting to consider the reasons for this. It is impossible to isolate and assess the relative importance of all the factors involved but three appear to stand out:

(i) Invergordon's known attractions
(ii) the support of the Highlands and Islands Development Board and regional policy in general
(iii) trends in the U.K. aluminium industry.

Firstly, the Invergordon area had long been recognised as an area suitable for industrial development. Specific proposals date back at least until the early 1940s. In 1942 the report of the Committee on Hydro-Electric Development in Scotland[1] identified potential areas for hydroelectric development which could generate industry growth and mentioned specifically East Ross. In 1945 the Association of Scientific Workers put forward similar views[2] and these were echoed by the 1948 White Paper on the distribution of industry which in relation to the scheduling of certain areas for development assistance stated that

"It would be inappropriate to schedule the whole of the Highlands and Islands as a Development area . . . in view of the prospects for industries using hydro-electricity, there is a case for making Development Area powers available in a district chosen because of its suitability as the focal centre of industrial development in the Highlands as a whole and not merely because of its local unemployment".[3]

The area identified was that surrounding the Cromarty and Beauly Firths and corresponding approximately to the Moray Firth Sub-Region. Although nothing happened subsequently the notion was not lost and reappeared in the 1965 White Paper on the Scottish economy[4] which proposed, inter alia, the establishment of three growth centres in the region — the Moray Firth, Caithness and Lochaber.

A major step forward occurred in 1965 with the establishment of the Highlands and Islands Development Board, the first body of its type in the U.K., charged with the economic and social regeneration of the Highlands and Islands. In its first annual report the Board enthusiastically accepted the notion of growth centres and began actively to try to put it into practice:

"Manufacturing industry is very poorly represented in the Highlands and Islands. Without it, the region will continue to lack any real possibility of a substantial enough rise in numbers to give credibility to Highland regeneration. Numbers are important in the justification or provision of all services internal to the Highlands and in major improvements in communications between the Highlands and the South.

---

[1] Cmd 6406 (London, 1942) para 44
[2] Association of Scientific Workers: *Highland Power* (London, 1945)
[3] Cmd 7540 (London, 1948)
[4] Cmnd 2864 (London, 1965)

Modern industrial enterprises are absolutely essential in providing more of the kind of skills and initiative which will breed new enterprises and broaden the range of social and cultural leadership. Our policy in this field is, therefore, threefold:

we encourage the growth of industrial enterprise wherever a developer shows a personal and specific desire to settle or expand his enterprise;

we will pursue, however, a more methodical programme of building small industrial growth points in scale with the possibilities of the West and islands;

we will do our utmost to generate major growth points, involving substantial increases in population wherever the natural advantages of the area seem to warrant it; the Moray Firth is unquestionably the most important of these areas."[5]

The Board's views for the Moray Firth areas were spelt out in some detail:

"to establish a major centre of modern job opportunity for those from within and without the Highlands, offering conditions in all respects comparable with the best likely to become available in United Kingdom;

to establish a major centre which can offer within the region a full range of modern commercial, social, cultural and other activities as well as job opportunity;

to demonstrate that enterprises founded in the Highlands are capable of thoroughly profitable operation without recourse to revenue subsidy;

to assist in the improvement of the U.K.'s balance of payments: the Moray Firth looks naturally to export markets just as much as to home markets;

to offer a "home market" of reasonable size for the region's products, such as food, which will strengthen the position of the primary producers of the area and give a sounder base for adding value locally to their products: it will also require, and provide a basis of demand for, improvements in transport and other social provisions as well as benefiting, and benefiting from, improvements in recreation and tourist facilities;

to help to balance the economic structure of the area in which the distinctive feature is the very small representation of manufacturing industry".[6]

In March 1966 the Board commissioned Product Planning Ltd. to carry out a study of the feasibility of industry development in the area. In December 1966 the Board made a formal submission to the Secretary of State for Scotland requesting support for additional studies and some of these studies were undertaken in 1967, concerning the physical planning implications, soil surveys, the feasibility of a deepwater pier and bulk-handling facilities and the possibility of generating cheap power for industrial use. The last-mentioned investigation led to a formal proposal to the Secretary of State which in the event did not come to fruition but probably had some influence on subsequent events.

The first serious discussions with a major firm were with Occidental Petroleum regarding the possibility of establishing an oil refinery in the vicinity of Invergordon but in the event they went to Canvey Island in the

[5] HIDB: *First Report* (Inverness, 1967) p.4
[6] Ibid, pp. 16-17

south of England. Then the Board heard that Alcan Aluminium, the large Canadian firm, were thinking of building an aluminium smelter in the U.K. and in the course of a trade mission to North America Board representatives held preliminary discussions with the company. Negotiations led to Alcan submitting an application for planning permission for a site near Invergordon, as also did British Aluminium, and it was the latter application which proved successful eventually, with Alcan going to North East England.

The aluminium industry in the U.K. has had a peculiar history and the events in the late 1960s were a major turning point. In the late 1950s and early 1960s the growth of worldwide aluminium demand was roughly 8% per year. In 1967 the United Kingdom consumption of aluminium products was 356,000 tons but only 39,000 tons of aluminium ingot were produced in the United Kingdom, the remainder being imported from Norway, Canada and elsewhere. As a consequence of various factors, some of the major aluminium producers in the world began to consider the possibility of constructing aluminium reduction plants (smelters) in the United Kingdom and the eventual outcome was the commissioning in 1971 of plant with a capacity of 260,000 tons per annum.

The production of aluminium requires four main processes. The first is the extraction, screening and drying of bauxite, the basic raw material. Bauxite is then converted to alumina (pure aluminium oxide), usually using the Bayer process. Thirdly, the alumina is electrolytically reduced to aluminium and, fourthly, the raw aluminium is converted into semi-manufactured forms sich as bars, sheets and strips for use by other industries.

Each of these four production processes has its peculiar location characteristics and requirements. The first stage — the extraction, screening and drying of bauxite — occurs inevitably at the source of the bauxite deposits, which are found mainly in the Caribbean, Latin America, Ghana, Surinam, Australia, Greece and France.

The second production stage — the conversion of bauxite to alumina — is undergone in alumina plants usually sited near the bauxite deposits. The main reason for this is that the process reduces by half the weight of the bauxite and source-orientated location consequently reduces transport costs. It is not unknown, however, for such plants to be located elsewhere, particularly if an alumina plant serves more than one reduction works.

In the present context the main interest is in the location of reduction plant, i.e. aluminium smelters. The locational characteristics of smelters are described in detail below but can be summarized here. The main cost factor in aluminium reduction is the power cost, which accounts for between 15% and 20% of the selling price. Power costs vary considerably with location and therefore smelters are usually located in areas of cheap power. In addition, in cases where smelters have to rely on imported bauxite it is necessary to site them in coastal locations with facilities for handling bulk cargoes. In certain countries — West Germany and Italy, for example — it was felt that considerations such as import saving and security of supply outweighed more commercial considerations of cost minimization and smelters have been located there, usually on the basis of subsidized power. More recently, some of the major aluminium producers have shown a tendency to locate new smelters close to the markets served.

The fourth production stage — the casting of aluminium into semi-manufactured or semi-fabricated forms — is almost always undertaken close to the markets (in industrial areas). Transport costs on semi-manufactured products are roughly twice those on aluminium ingot.

Outside the communist bloc, the industry is largely controlled by six vertically integrated companies which own most of the known bauxite reserves, produce most of the world's alumina and aluminium, and fabricate a large proportion of final output. The six companies (with, in parenthesis, their share of 1967 reduction capacity) are Alcan Aluminium Ltd. (17.6%), the Aluminium Company of America (Alcoa) (16.9%), Reynolds Metals Company (13.0%), Kaiser Aluminium and Chemical Corporation (10.9%), Pechiney Chemical and Electrometall-urgical Company (7.1%) and Schweizerisches Aluminium A.G. (Alusuisse) (5.4%). Obviously, the actions of these six companies determine the development of the aluminium industry.[7]

In 1967, United Kingdom consumption of primary aluminium totalled 356,000 tons compared with domestic production of 39,000 tons.[8] The latter was the output of two small smelters owned by the British Aluminium Company (a jointly-owned subsidiary of Reynolds Metals and Tube Investments) and located at Lochaber and Kinlochleven in the Scottish Highlands. Built to use the cheap hydro-electric power then available in the western Highlands, the smelters began production in 1909 and 1929 respectively. In fact British Aluminium was established in 1894 with a small smelter at Foyers, also in the Highlands, which closed in 1967. Three other smelters have also existed in the United Kingdom but have long since ceased production.

The United Kingdom imported 307,000 tons of primary aluminium in 1967, most of that coming from Norway (106,000 tons) and Canada (123,000 tons). Brubaker wrote in 1967 that "Great Britain is the outstanding example of a country that departs from a self-sufficiency position. The British impose no tariff on ingot yet maintain a substantial fabricating industry for which they are able to obtain imported metal at competitive prices . . . the United Kingdom is anxious to get its metal at low cost and seemingly has no aspirations to produce more of its own. Competition in this country is felt in the semis market"[9]

For a number of reasons, however, some of the major aluminium producers began in the mid 1960s to examine the possibilities of building new smelters in the United Kingdom and there was increasing government support for an expansion of domestic reduction capacity. The factors can be classified into two groups — general ones, affecting the industry as a whole, and factors specific to particular companies. Eight main reasons for the general change of attitude can be identified:
    (i) the growth of demand for aluminium

---

[7] A detailed account of the structure of the aluminium industry can be found in S. Brubaker: *Trends in the world aluminium industry* (Baltimore, 1967).
[8] Tables 3.1 to 3.3 summarize the main statistical information relevant to the decisions outlined in this chapter.
[9] Ibid, pages 135 and 240

(ii) a tendency to site smelters nearer their markets
(iii) the possibility of cheaper electricity in the United Kingdom
(iv) over-capacity and instability in the semi-manufacturing sector
(v) potential membership of the European Economic Community
(vi) the United Kingdom's balance of payments problems
(vii) increasing fears of foreign domination in the aluminium industry
(viii) increasing pressure for more effective regional policies.

These reasons are briefly discussed below; comments on the involvement of the particular companies involved are towards the end of this section.

The first two reasons have been covered above. World consumption of aluminium had been growing at around 8% per year and demand in the United Kingdom was increasing at a slightly faster rate. Changing commercial considerations and political pressures were altering locational characteristics in such a way as to make market locations attractive.

The major reason why so little aluminium was produced in the United Kingdom was the high cost of power. Hydro-electric power in the Highlands was produced at around 0.3d[10] per unit but this would not now be true for new plant. In Canada and the United States smelters dependent on hydro-electric power obtained their electricity at between 0.2d and 0.3d per unit; in Norway the equivalent figure was between 0.3d and 0.4d; whilst the bulk tariff in the United Kingdom was around 0.8d per unit. It was generally recognised that it would be unprofitable to produce aluminium with electricity over 0.4d per unit. The United Kingdom was consequently at a substantial disadvantage compared with North America and Norway, but the advent of nuclear generating stations offered the chance of eliminating this cost disadvantage. A government White Paper published in 1965[11] claimed that an advanced gas — cooled reactor (AGR) was expected to produce electricity at a cost of 0.5d per unit, substantially cheaper than coal or oil-fired power stations. Although this figure was still above the minimum cost on which the industry operated, the possibility of cost reductions in related spheres of aluminium reduction (principally through government grants for capital investment) significantly altered the situation.

In addition, the lack of reduction capacity was not mirrored in the semi-manufacturing sector where there was evidence of substantial over-capacity. Although British Aluminium was the only primary producer in the United Kingdom, it had many competitors in the semi-manufacturing sector, notably Alcan and Alcoa and two independents, Impalco and James Booth. Competition among these firms and the need to replace outdated plant had resulted in over-capacity and the producing companies outside the United Kingdom were acutely aware of the need to secure their outlets. If one company were able to obtain lower-cost aluminium (e.g. through government grants for a domestic smelter), the others would be obliged to follow suit. Also, the profits in the semi-manufacturing sector were low (and frequently negative) and, because the reduction stage is probably the most profitable stage in the aluminium industry, the construction of smelters was becoming more attractive. The managing director of British Aluminium was quoted as saying that the company

---

[10] i.e. old pence. Costs are at their 1967 levels.
[11] Cmnd 2798: *Fuel Policy* (London, 1965)

21

Table 3.1 — World production of primary aluminium, 1967-72

thousand metric tons

	1967	1968	1969	1970	1971	1972
Europe						
Austria	78.8	85.9	89.7	91.4	90.0	84.0
France	361.2	365.7	371.7	381.0	375.0	392.4
Germany F.R.	252.9	257.5	262.7	309.3	427.5	434.4
Greece	71.6	76.3	81.7	88.4	111.0	129.9
Iceland	—	6	8.7	38.4	41.0	45.5
Italy	127.7	142.2	143.6	146.7	136.4	149.5
Netherlands	32.1	49.1	72.1	75.7	116.3	166.4
Norway	362.8	462.8	501.6	530.2	528.6	542.2
Spain	78.5	89.3	106.4	119.1	125.4	146.0
Sweden	33.4	56.8	66.8	66.2	75.5	77.6
Switzerland	72.3	75.8	77.1	91.8	93.9	83.6
United Kingdom	39.0	38.2	33.8	39.6	119.0	171.4
Yugoslavia	44.6	48.1	48.4	47.7	46.6	58.4
Total	1554.9	1747.7	1864.3	2025.5	2286.2	2481.3
Africa	88.0	155.9	159.8	165.4	191.2	233.7
Asia	493.9	622.0	730.0	932.8	1118.7	1320.6
America	3933.1	3960.0	4573.5	4748.7	4774.9	4861.6
of which Canada	873.9	888.3	978.6	972.2	1016.9	918.0
U.S.A.	2965.8	2952.9	3441.0	3607.1	3560.9	3737.6
Australasia	92.8	97.3	126.4	205.6	245.9	292.7
Other countries*	1783.4	1932.5	2020.7	2143.1	2253.3	2340.2
World Total	7946.1	8515.4	9474.7	10,221.1	10,870.2	11,530.1

* Figures for communist-bloc countries are estimates
Source: World Metal Statistics

Table 3.2 — World consumption of aluminium, 1967-72

	1967	1968	1969	1970	1971	1972
Europe						
Austria	60.5	68.9	70.0	82.3	72.7	70.0
France	294.0	293.5	367.1	413.3	377.4	398.3
Germany F.R.	416.8	539.5	642.3	589.6	609.6	724.4
Greece	11.1	14.4	15.1	29.3	27.0	25.0
Iceland	—	—	—	—	—	—
Italy	184.0	217.0	258.0	279.0	254.0	300.0
Netherlands	26.4	31.4	53.4	50.4	59.9	72.0
Norway	39.3	54.0	68.1	80.0	83.0	97.0
Spain	78.2	98.2	128.1	129.1	150.4	170.0
Sweden	53.4	62.1	76.4	78.7	79.0	86.4
Switzerland	59.3	67.2	81.2	99.7	85.2	90.0
United Kingdom	355.8	387.7	387.7	404.2	325.6	409.9
Yugoslavia	70.0	61.2	73.0	76.0	80.0	80.0
Other Europe	155.9	181.7	198.0	222.2	226.5	228.7
Total	1804.7	2076.8	2418.4	2533.8	2430.3	2751.7
Africa	32.1	40.7	60.2	69.1	75.0	80.0
Asia	704.3	833.7	1037.2	1045.2	1193.5	1511.4
America	3431.8	3948.8	4114.2	3913.6	4393.3	4754.3
of which Canada	166.1	187.9	212.5	222.9	254.9	230.0
U.S.A.	3119.2	3597.1	3706.2	3488.0	3916.1	4296.3
Australasia	92.5	113.8	117.7	127.6	153.0	126.5
Other countries*	1695.0	1838.0	1915.8	1993.1	2133.2	2250.2
World Total	7760.4	8851.8	9663.5	9682.4	10,378.3	11,473.9

* Figures for communist-bloc countries are estimates
Source: World Metal Statistics.

Talbe 3.3 — Self-sufficiency ratios

	1967	percentages 1972
Europe	86.2	90.2
Austria	129.4	120.0
France	122.9	98.5
Germany F.R.	60.7	60.0
Greece	650.9	519.6
Italy	69.4	49.8
Netherlands	121.6	231.1
Norway	923.2	559.0
Spain	99.7	85.9
Sweden	62.5	89.8
Switzerland	121.9	92.9
United Kingdom	11.0	41.8
Yugoslavia	63.7	73.0
Canada	526.1	399.1
U.S.A.	95.1	87.0

believed that "having its own large smelter means that the company will have a much closer control over its supplies of metal, which will be beneficial to its fabricating activities."[12]

The fifth reason for the upsurge of interest in smelters was the interest shown by the three major political parties in membership of the European Economic Community. In the mid 1960s the external tariff imposed on aluminium by the Community was 9%; West German smelters had largely grown up behind this tariff; and demand for aluminium in the Community was growing at a faster than average rate. The interest shown by Norway in joining the Community strengthened these considerations, because if Norway joined and the United Kingdom did not imports would suffer substantially.

The remaining reasons relate to the increased interest shown by the Labour Government which had come to power in 1964 and strengthened

---

[12] *Western Mail*, 23rd October 1968.

its position in the 1966 election. During the 1960s one of the major objectives of United Kingdom economic policy was to obtain a satisfactory balance on the balance of payments. Government ministers were therefore receptive to proposals for import substitution and as imports of primary aluminium totalled about £55 millions per year they were an obvious target. There was also concern at the extent of foreign domination in the domestic aluminium industry. In the late 1950s a number of United Kingdom firms lost their independence as Reynolds, Kaiser and Alcoa substantially extended their operations. The result was strong political pressure for a larger domestic aluminium industry.

One of the Government's other main economic objectives was to try to reduce regional disparities within the country. Regional policies had existed in various forms for many years but during the early 1960s regional disparities — particularly in unemployment levels — increased significantly. In pursuance of this policy objective, the Government introduced in 1966 the Industrial Development Act. Part 1 of the Act empowered the Board of Trade to make investment grants towards approved capital expenditure. The standard rate was 20% but in development areas (mainly Scotland, Wales, and the north of England) the rate was 40%.[13] Aluminium smelters were eligible for grants under the Act and the prospect of 40% grants for plant and machinery were very attractive to the aluminium companies. From the Government's point of view the Act, together with other regional policy legislation, offered strong inducements to increase employment in the development areas.

The origins of any tangible expression of these changing factors can be traced back to 1962. In that year Rio-Tinto Zinc, the large mining group, were known to be investigating the possibility of building a smelter in the United Kingdom but nothing materialized. Three years later, in the light of the published statements on nuclear reactors, the company renewed its interest and held preliminary discussions with the Atomic Energy Authority. Other companies followed suit and it is known that at least one put forward firm proposals (Alcan to the Scottish Office in May 1967).

The event which marked the beginning of detailed negotiations, however, was the announcement in October 1967 of government support for the construction of domestic reduction capacity. On the 4th October, at the annual conference of the Labour Party, the Prime Minister, Mr. Harold Wilson, said that:[14]

"As a result of great advances in nuclear generation, where Britain now leads the world . . . the new nuclear generating stations of the 1970s will be able to provide electricity for industrial use far cheaper than electricity costs today . . . This will mean that it will be economic to establish big new industries in this country which we have not had before because our power costs were not competitive with hydro-electric power overseas. And it will mean the opportunity, in Development Areas, for new industries which we have not previously had in this country. Industries which will help to make us less dependent on overseas production. We are now

---

[13] The rates were increased to 25% and 45% respectively for approved expenditure incurred between 1st January 1967 and 31st December 1968.
[14] *Report of the 66th Annual Conference of the Labour Party, Scarborough, 1967* (London 1967) pp. 218 - 219.

25

prepared to build publicly-owned power stations to work in partnership with private enterprise smelter industries — the electricity to be supplied at a price based on the stations' own generating costs. And the construction can start now. We are ready to start today to discuss with the aluminium industry the provision of one or more giant smelters, competitively powered with nuclear energy . . . there is a possibility — which I am now discussing with the Chairman of the Coal Board — of associating the coal industry with this type of project in the Development Areas."

In the months which followed this announcement, four companies submitted detailed proposals to the Government: Alcan, Alusuisse, British Aluminium and Rio-Tinto Zinc/British Insulated Callander Cables Aluminium Holdings. RTZ/BICC and British Aluminium both proposed 120,000 ton nuclear-powered smelters; Alcan and Alusuisse proposed 60,000 ton smelters based on coal-fired schemes. The Government passed the proposals to the Industrial Reorganisation Corporation to undertake an evaluation and a report was received in January 1968. It is understood that the Industrial Reorganisation Corporation expressed reservations about the coal-fired smelters, largely on the grounds of size, but in principle there was general support. Legislation was introduced in Parliament after discussions with other interested parties, including the European Free Trade Association, Norway and Canada, and the 1968 Industrial Expansion Act formed the basis of government assistance to the industry. The main assistance was in the form of favourable fuel supply arrangements, set out in a White Paper,[15] and the benefits and implications of those have been discussed critically elsewhere.[16] The negotiations with the countries providing the bulk of existing imports led to some modifications in the companies' proposals: the four original proposals were for a total annual capacity of 360,000 tons, compared with the 260,000 tons capacity that has actually come onstream. The eventual outcome also implied a compromise benefiting the three main development areas, which was reminiscent of the steel strip mills in the 1950s.[17]

In terms of the locations of the three smelters finally approved, it was understood from the outset of negotiations that any smelters which might be established would be located in development areas. The existence of substantial investment grants in such areas made this a condition very acceptable to the aluminium companies. Subject to that condition, the companies were free to propose sites based upon their commercial judgement. All four companies surveyed a number of sites but Alusuisse soon dropped their interest. British Aluminium visited eighteen sites in the United Kingdom and chose a short list of five: Invergordon, Hunterston, Graythorpe (Teesside), Blyth and Milford Haven. Invergordon was their first choice, despite considerable Scottish pressure for Hunterston. Rio-Tinto Zinc undertook detailed examinations of six sites — Anglesey, Invergordon, Fife, two sites in South West Scotland and one in Ulster — and expressed a strong preference for Anglesey. Alcan really only considered Invergordon and this told against them in the discussions

[15] Cmnd 3819: *Industrial investment: the production of primary aluminium* (London, 1968)
[16] See S. Ash: *The U.K. primary aluminium industry: a case study in non-tariff barriers* (London, 1972)
[17] G. Manners: *Misplacing the smelters* in *New Society,* 16th May, 1968, pp. 712-713

consequential upon British Aluminium's choice of the same location.

The British Aluminium and RTZ/BICC choices quickly received Government approval. Alcan's desire for a smelter at Invergordon using coal from North East England caused many problems and the outcome was the transfer of their site to Lynemouth, in North East England.

British Aluminium began construction of its 100,000 ton smelter in December 1968 and production commenced in May 1971. The £40 million plant was constructed by Taywood Wrightson, a joint company set up by Taylor Woodrow Construction Ltd. and Head Wrightson Ltd., to act as managing contractors. The project was completed on time and within the budget.

The Anglesey smelter came onstream in December 1970. The 100,000 ton smelter cost around £50 million and is operated by Anglesey Aluminium Metal Ltd., an operating company jointly formed by Rio-Tinto Zinc, British Insulated Callenders Cables and Kaiser Anglesey Aluminium employ around 800 people.

Alcan did not begin production until July 1972, some eighteen months behind schedule. The 60,000 ton first stage and the power station together cost nearly £45 million. Serious construction delays arose through disputes among the contractors and certain trade unions (mainly concerning the power station) and at one stage an investigation was undertaken by the Commission on Industrial Relations.[18] Alcan presently employ around 600 men (including 100 in the power station) and in addition the jobs of nearly 1,000 miners at the Lynemouth colliery have been guaranteed.

Earlier, the general reasons for the increase in U.K. aluminium production were outlined. It would now be appropriate to consider briefly the factors specifically affecting the British Aluminium decision. Both British Aluminium and Alcan obviously had defensive market reasons for following RTZ's plans to build a smelter in the United Kingdom. Also, over the years British Aluminium had sought to secure the ingot supplies. Because of the high cost of domestic power supplies, previous expansion had taken place overseas, specifically at Baie Comeau in Canada where a 100,000 tonnes smelter came onstream in 1957 and which supplied the company's fabrication plants in the United Kingdom. The Baie Comeau smelter, however, had many disadvantages. It was only partly owned by British Aluminium (having been built in partnership with a non-aluminium company sharing the power supply) and the company's share of the profits was subject to higher Canadian taxes before it reached the United Kingdom; the metal was bought for United Kingdom operations at a fixed price near the top end of the market scale; there was the impending 9% E.E.C. tariff facing Canadian exports; and the various problems associated with long supply lines. Full control and shorter supply lines were very attractive to the company and the Invergordon smelter provided the answer. Since Invergordon began production, British Aluminium has sold its 50% stake in the Baie Comeau smelter to Reynolds, which has consequently postponed its own plans for expanding reduction capacity and has taken up the 65,000 tonnes per annum that British Aluminium imported from Canada. This has meant that the company continues to

---

[18] Commission on Industrial Relations, Report No. 29: *Alcan smelter site* (London, 1972)

import from Norway — from the DNN smelter it shares with Alcan — at a rate of around 20,000 tonnes per annum.

Reverting to the situation in East Ross, the Alcan and British Aluminium applications raised important planning issues because the land was zoned for agricultural use in the County Development Plan. Consequently, Ross and Cromarty County Council put forward Amendment No. 3 to the plan for the rezoning of 736 acres of land east of Invergordon (consisting largely of the farms of Inverbreakie and Ord) for industrial use and 165 acres at Alness for housing. The Secretary of State for Scotland decided that a public inquiry would be necessary and this was held in Dingwall in February and March 1968.

Although there was a strong body of opinion in favour of industrial development, there was also strong and well organized opposition, led by farmers in the area who objected to the loss of good agricultural land and, inter alia, suggested as an alternative that Nigg Bay be reclaimed for industrial use. Evidence in support of the amendment was given by the County Council, the H.I.D.B., Alcan and British Aluminium. In his report to the Secretary of State the Reporter at the inquiry, W. Munro, recommended approval of the amendment because industrial development would be beneficial to the local economy, and welcomed by most people, and because the loss of agricultural land would be comparatively small. The Secretary of State accepted the recommendation and approval was given in June 1968. Subsequently, in July the County Council granted to British Aluminium planning permission in principle to build an aluminium smelter at Inverbreakie Farm near Invergordon and a few weeks later the Government gave it approval, stating that Alcan would have to find an alternative site. As was discussed above, they went to Lynemouth in England.

It must be stressed that the British Aluminium development cannot be considered in isolation from other changes occurring in East Ross and that some knowledge of these is required. Some of these are dealt with in more detail later in this report but a brief summary would probably be helpful at this juncture.

In October 1968 Grampian Chemicals applied for permission to build a petrochemical plant on the farms of Pollo and Delney, to the east of Ord Farm. Again the County Council were in favour and proposed another amendment (No. 6) to the Development Plan. A public inquiry was held from February to April 1969 and the Reporter, F.W. O'Brien, recommended rejection largely on the grounds that Nigg Bay could be reclaimed for the use required. The Secretary of State, however, gave approval and rezoned the 1,094 acres adjoining the area already zoned and a further 367 acres on the east side of Nigg Bay. This amendment made no provision for additional land for housing and in 1971 the County Council submitted an application for Amendment 7 to rezone 340 acres of agricultural land around Alness for housing and related infrastructure. Another public inquiry was held in May of that year and the Reporter, J.R. Fiddes, submitted his report in December 1972, recommending approval with the exception of one farm which he thought would be an unjustifiable loss of good agricultural land. This was accepted by the Secretary of State.

More recently, other amendments to the County Development Plan have increased the land zoned for industry and housing and in 1972 the County Council published a "Planning Strategy for Easter Ross", outlining their long-term proposals. Since then Highlands Fabricators have established a large oil production platform year at Nigg and MK-Shand a pipecoating yard at Invergordon, and there have been other oil-related developments in the area, including three other sites zoned for platform construction but at which no work has begun. The implications of these developments for the aluminium smelter and the local economy in general are discussed in more detail, where appropriate, later in this report.[19]

---

[19] See Chapters 7-9. For a discussion of the main planning issues see also A. Currie and associates: *The objectives of Highland development: an Easter Ross case study* (Lamington, 1973) and G.A. Mackay: *Prospects for the Moray Firth sub-region* (Aberdeen 1975)

4 Growth Centre Policies

The existence and identification of differential rates of regional economic growth, particularly in developed economies, have led to the development of a number of theories which attempt to explain such spatial imbalances. In most aspects of regional economics, the pragmatic and policy-oriented nature of research has contributed haphazardly to the construction of an appropriate body of theory. In effect, this can bring about a vicious circle in that many regional policies have been founded on imperfect knowledge and little theoretical support.

Within the scope of regional economics, one of the best examples of this process of an inadequate theoretical construct being translated into a common policy tool is the notion of the growth centre. The terminology is in itself imprecise and is variously construed to include growth poles, growth points, development poles, industrial complexes, industrial estates etc.

As described briefly in the preceding chapter, a policy of establishing growth centres in the Highlands has been one objective of the H.I.D.B. In that light, and in view of the need to be able to assess the success of various regional policies, it would be sensible at this point to examine the constituent elements of growth centre theory in some detail in order that in the concluding chapter an assessment of the role of the Invergordon smelter can be made.

In recent years growth centre theory and policies have attracted considerable attention and a number of authors have demonstrated a need for synthesis and more rigorous theoretical and methodological formulation.[1] For example, Hermansen has recently written that: "Although the original concept of development poles was envisaged as a tool to study the anatomy of economic development in abstract economic space, in the course of time its scope has been considerably broadened and the theory underlying it generalized so that both the concept and the theory can now be said to deal synthetically with the problem of societal development — as opposed to economic progress — in a simultaneous sectoral-spatial-temporal setting."

"A consequence of both the generalization of the theory and the increased popularity and use of the concepts as catchwords in the political discussion of regional problems has been that the theory has lost much of its original content and meaning, and the concepts have become gradually more and more elusive and ill-suited for empirical testing and practical sicentific application."[2]

Although any classification of the theory into constituent elements is in principle unrealistic and partially arbitrary, it is felt that in this instance

---

[1] See, for example: T. Hermansen: *Development poles and development centres in national and regional development* in A.R. Kuklinski (ed): *Growth poles and growth centres in national and regional planning* (The Hague, 1972); N.M. Hansen: *Intermediate-size cities as growth centres* (New York, 1971)

[2] T. Hermansen, op. cit., pp. 1 - 2

there are advantages in so doing. Most writers attribute the origins of the theory to the works of Francois Perroux, who in an article published in 1955 observed that "growth does not appear everywhere at the same time; it appears in growth points or growth poles with varying intensity; it advances by different channels and with varying final effects for the whole economy,"[3] Since then Perroux' work has been modified, reformulated and integrated with other (similar) theories. For present purposes, five main elements of the theory of growth centres can be identified. It should be stressed that these are not exhaustive nor necessarily exclusive. The five elements are:

(i) the 'French school'
(ii) the theory of unbalanced growth
(iii) industrial complex theory
(iv) central place theory
(v) the theory of information diffusion.

The members of the 'French school' are taken to be the group of French and Belgian economists who adopted and developed Perroux' seminal work throughout the late 1950s and 1960s. Perroux' main interest was in the declining industrial areas of France and West Germany in which some firms and industries were growing rapidly while most declined. He suggested that the most important factor causing these different experiences was the adoption and diffusion of innovations and in this sense, he regarded development as the introduction and diffusion of successive waves of innovations which were the mechanisms through which economic growth and structural change occurred. His definition of space has resulted in considerable confusion regarding the notions of growth poles and growth centres, a confusion exacerbated by mistranslations and semantic inconsistencies of subsequent writers. It is clearly evident, however, that Perroux was not concerned with geographic space and, as regards economic space, he distinguished three types: economic space as a plan, as a field of forces and as a homogeneous entity. It was left to others, notably Boudeville[4], to translate these concepts into economic space.

In giving the earlier work a spatial framework, Perroux was concerned with the second of the above types, i.e. economic space in its functional form. "As a field of forces economic space consists of centres (or poles, or foci) from which centrifugal forces emanate and to which centripetal forces are attracted."[5] These effects were exercised by economic units, regarding which Perroux distinguished between propulsive firms or industries (firmes ou industries motrice) and attracted firms or industries (firmes ou industries entrainee). The important features of the former were their large size, complex interindustry relationships and their membership of fast-growing industries. Other members of the French school have subsequently expanded on these basic principles of the concept of dominance.

---

[3] F. Perroux: *"Note sur la notion de pole de croissance", Economic appliquee,* nos. 1 - 2, January - June 1955

[4] J.R. Boudeville: *Problems of regional economic planning* (Edinburgh, 1966), pp. 1 - 21

[5] F. Perroux: *Economic space: theory and applications,* op. cit., p. 91

One final point to stress regarding the French school concerns the notion of space. Perroux' concept of the growth pole related to abstract topological space. Boudeville has translated Perroux' three types of economic space into geographic space, distinguishing among homogeneous, polarized and planning regions[6], and it is with the existence of economic phenomena in polarized regions that growth pole theorists have been concerned. The importance of the mathematical transformation of economic space into geographic space has been missed by certain writers and the confusion between growth poles and growth centres is a consequence of that. In the present context, the definitions used are that growth poles exist in economic space and growth centres in geographic space.

The observation of geographic differentials in economic growth and welfare is a fundamental element of the second contributory theoretical group, namely the unbalanced growth school. Although the work of the three main proponents (Hirschman, Myrdal and Friedmann) has been mainly concerned with underdeveloped countries, there are similarities with underdeveloped areas of developed countries. Hirschman has argued that development should be concentrated in certain industrial sectors and geographical areas for, on the basis of his Latin American experience, "there can be little doubt that an economy to lift itself to higher income levels must and will first develop within itself one or several centres of economic strength."[7] His belief was that the potential for growth would be dissipated by attempts to spread development evently among sectors and regions. If development were concentrated in selected centres, it would set in motion 'trickling down' forces which would induce development in the hinterlands of the centres through an increased demand for the products of the hinterlands and through the transfer of capital. Hirschman observed, however, that there would also be unfavourable 'polarization'[8] effects in that the hinterlands would suffer as a result of competition from the centres (particularly as transportation facilities improved) and that they would experience some loss of savings and the able labour force.

Myrdal's theory of cumulative causation is closely related to the above. Myrdal maintained that the free play of market forces tended to increase rather than decrease regional inequalities. "The localities and regions where economic activity is expanding will attract net immigration from other parts of the country. As migration is always selective, at least with respect to the migrant's age, this movement by itself tends to favour the rapidly growing communities and disfavour the others"[9] Such inflows of capital and labour would boost local demand in the growth centres sufficient to attract new firms, there would be increased expenditure on infrastructure and social capital which in turn would induce conditions more favourable to invention and innovation . . . and so on.

Myrdal identified two types of effect of such concentrations, 'spread' effects and 'backwash' effects, which are synonymous with Hirschman's trickling down and polarization effects, respectively. Myrdal was more pessimistic

[6] J. R. Boudeville, op. cit.

[7] A.O. Hirschman: *The strategy of economic development* (New Haven, 1958)

[8] Polarization not in the French sense but in the English sense of increasing differences.

[9] G. Myrdal: *Economic theory and underdeveloped regions* (London, 1957), p. 27

in so far as he believed that the movements of labour and capital were more important than the interregional trade effects.

The work of Friedmann on regional problems in Venezuela[10] can also be considered in this context. Essentially, Friedmann regarded intraregional differences as taking the form of a core-periphery division. His concern was with a basically 'colonial' country, with a centre (core) on the coast and a periphery from which resources were exported, by way of the centre, to the colonizing country overseas. Other relationships between the centre and the periphery were negligible. Friedmann observed that growth usually occurred in cities and towns because of agglomeration economies and suggested that there was a strong relationship between city size and rate of growth. In this he came close to the central place theories of Christaller and others.

One other parallel that can be drawn from Friedmann's work is with export-base theory, for Friedmann stressed that the essential concomitant of economic growth was export demand. Successful translation of the export sector into domestic growth depended on social and political structures and the reponsiveness of local entrepreneurs. Consequently, any loss of entrepreneurial ability in the periphery reduced the extent to which the periphery was capable of sharing in the growth of the core because of the lessened ability to adopt innovations diffused from the core. Alternatively, the core would consolidate its dominance through the polarization effects outlined above.

The third contributory element to growth centre theory is industrial complex theory. This element draws together the concepts of polarization and agglomeration effects. A simple definition of an industrial complex is that of a group of firms or industries, located close together, which have important technical and economic linkages. The main feature is this existence of interrelations which distinguish an industrial complex from similar industrial agglomerations which are not technically related. Such a distinction draws heavily on the existence of external economies and, indirectly, economies of large-scale production, both consequences of the increased specialization of production. If manufacturers specialize in the production of one particular item, which may only be a component of a larger item, they are very dependent on other manufacturers. "In order to produce, a manufacturer must have close at hand all the intermediary industries: sub-contractors, i.e. firms concerned at one stage or another in the manufacture of a specific article, and suppliers of services, in particular those whose function is installation and maintenance of plant. None of this intermediary work will be a paying proposition if it is done for a single customer. Each intermediary manufacturer must devote himself to one operation only, but he must do this for a large number of user industries. Only then can he obtain the production level necessary to bring his costs down low enough to justify his existence. Consequently, it is quite clear that for complex-cycle industries an entrepreneur can only reasonably envisage manufacturing a finished product in centres where he can find all the industries auxiliary to his own. Conversely, a subcontractor or supplier

[10] J. Friedmann: *Regional development policy: a case study of Venezuela* (Cambridge, Mass., 1966)

of services will only set up in an area with an adequate market in the shape of firms requiring his specialized services."[11]

The polarization effects of this concentration are in the main the economies of scale and interdependence, arising from interfirm or inter-industry transactions and joint demand for or supply of products and services. These interfirm or interindustry linkages can be forward, backward or horizontal. An example given by Isard[12] is of a complex of firms mining coal and iron ore, subsequently producing pig iron and steel, and finally fabricating steel products: each successive activity constituting at least part of the market for the immediately preceding activity, and the converse.

The localization (agglomeration) economies arise through joint use of common facilities and resources (particularly infrastructure and labour), reductions in communication costs, the shortening of supply lines and the lessening of stock capacity requirements etc.

The proponents of industrial complex theory have suggested that such economies could be obtained by a systematic identification of interrelated industries and their establishment in a common location. The inherent implication of planning has made industrial complex theory more popular in centrally planned economies than elsewhere, but it has attracted attention and attempts have been made to establish complexes in certain Western economies, such as Italy.

A fourth contributory element to growth centre theory is central place theory. This body of theory has mainly been the domain of geographers and economic geographers, and can be regarded as deductive rather than inductive in that it is based on empirical observation of existing patterns. The origins of this work can be traced back to the first half of this century and in particular to the work of Christaller[13] and Losch[14]. The underlying notion is that spatial organizations are subject to a set of ordering principles.

Four main principles form the basis of classical central place theory. Firstly, there is the tendency of mass to crystallize around a nucleus: this applies to most forms of matter and can easily be seen in human settle-ments. Secondly, each settlement has a particular function and importance and can be distinguished by the goods and services it provides. Thirdly, each good or service has its relevant hinterland or market area, with different goods having differing market areas. Fourthly, larger settlements provide more numerous and more important goods and services than smaller settlements, thus forming a hierarchy of settlements (higher order, lower order) and a hierarchy of goods and services. Higher order centres perform all the functions of lower order centres in addition to purely higher order functions.

---

[11] European Economic Community: *Study for the promotion of an industrial development pole in southern Italy* (Brussels, 1966), p.8

[12] W. Isard: *Methods of regional analysis* (Cambridge, Mass., 1960), p.37

[13] W. Christaller: *Central places in southern Germany* (Englewood Cliffs, 1965). The original German edition was published in 1933.

[14] A. Losch *The economics of location* (New Haven, 1954). The original German edition was published in 1940.

From the above it can be seen that the two important concepts are the ranges and threshold of the goods and services. The range is the area of influence from which a good or service attracts custom; the threshold is the minimum population (or income) size required to support the production of a good (for local consumption) or the provision of a service. A simple example of this hierarchical structure would be that it requires a town and hinterland of 10,000 population to support a secondary school, of 30,000 to support a hospital, of 50,000 to support a technical college and of 100,000 for a theatre. It would therefore be unlikely to find located and unprofitable to locate a particular service in a town which had less than the required threshold population, including the relevant hinterland. A similar hierarchy can be established for manufactured products.

It can be said that central place theory partially complements growth pole theory in that it is a general theory of location which stresses the geographic polarization of human settlements, albeit in a static framework. It is also related to the notion of optimal size of towns and cities, which takes into account more economic considerations such as external economies [15]

Finally, the fifth contributory element to growth centre theory identified earlier is the theory of information diffusion. Although one of the most important elements in growth theory generally, it has been consistently undervalued by economists. Perroux, in fact, did stress the importance of the diffusion and adoption of innovations in the growth of certain industrial sectors but the main stimulus, however, has come from the work of Hagerstrand in the early 1950s. [16]

Hagerstrand identified three important processes — the inventive creation of innovations, the diffusion of information about such innovations and their eventual adoption. Information is disseminated through certain channels, of which the most vital are the mass media and interpersonal contacts. Flows of information through and along these channels are regulated by the existence of barriers (physical, social, cultural) which on occasion can limit the geographical area of dissemination. Over time, there will emerge a hierarchical system of flows, for example, on national, regional and local levels. Hagerstrand's work suggested these flows and fields of communication are relatively stable.

There is obviously a parallel here with central place hierarchies and it is usually accepted that information coming into a region will in the first instance be received by the largest settlement. In cities the size and cultural milieu of the population, the range of firms and organization, the relative superiority of transport and other communications are all more conducive to information dissemination than in smaller settlements. [17]

Capital and labour flows largely depend on information flows. If economic growth is stimulated by the adoption of innovations then this growth will in turn bring about conditions more favourable to inventive

[15] See K. Allen: *Growth centres and growth centre policy* in European Free Trade Association: *Regional policy in EFTA*. (Edinburgh, 1968)

[16] T. Hagerstrand: *The propagation of innovation waves* (Lund, 1952) and also *Aspects of the spatial structure of social communication and the diffusion of information, Papers and Proceedings of the Regional Science Association* (1966).

[17] See W. Thompson: *A preface to urban economics* (Baltimore, 1965)

creation. Information flows can consequently be regarded as a type of external economy, which should permit a more rigorous integration of the theory of information diffusion with theories of regional economic growth. Growth centre theory as presently formulated does allow this, albeit in an incomplete framework.

Turning to growth centre policies in practice, since the pioneering work of Perroux many government and other development agencies have seen such policies as an important instrument of regional policy, enabling them in the first place to increase the rate of national economic growth and in the second place to reduce some regional inequalities. One implicit assumption has been that the spread or trickling down effects of growth centres have been much greater than the backwash or polarization effects.

It appears to be a reasonable generalization that in many cases where growth centre policies have been adopted, the agency responsible has not really had a clear understanding of what the formulation and implement- ation of such policies actually involved. It should be obvious from the earlier theoretical discussion that such confusion is not surprising, given that the theoretical basis is diffuse and far from clear. In some cases, particularly in the United Kingdom, it has been very difficult, indeed probably impossible, to identify the measures which the growth centre policies comprised. The inevitable corollary is that it has been impossible to evaluate the success or otherwise of the measures, not knowing what the policies actually entailed.

In the last two or three years there is evidence to suggest that, at least among the developed countries of Western Europe, growth centres as an instrument of regional policy have lost much of the attraction they had in the late 1960s and early 1970s. Their inherent vagueness and immeasur- ability are undoubtedly the major reasons for this demise. Also, a common problem has been that the agencies involved have not had all the necessary powers, for instance in the provision of improved infrastructure a la Christaller and Losch which frequently has been the responsibility of another authority not committed to a growth centre strategy. It would be tangential, therefore, to describe in any detail the policies that have been tried in Britain and elsewhere.

Nevertheless, one objective of this report is to try to assess the role of the Invergordon aluminium smelter as a major contributor to the establish- ment of a growth centre in the Moray Firth area, in the form that such a policy was put forward in the late 1960s. The concluding chapter, Chapter 9, deals with the more fundamental issue of whether or not the policies adopted comprised a growth centre policy in the sense that regional economic theory leads us to understand.

5 The input-output model

There are quite a few alternative approaches to impact analysis and the one chosen for this study was the construction of an input-output model of the East Ross economy. One of the common objectives of any impact study is the calculation of multipliers to show the increases in output, income or employment and input-output model can be used for this purpose. There are three main types of regional multipliers — export-base, Keynesian and input-output — and the last-named has certainly been the least popular in the U.K. Export-base multipliers are often used in the United States but data shortages in the U.K. have precluded its use on any significant scale. Instead, frequent use has been made of a regional version of the Keynesian foreign trade multiplier but a disadvantage is that this is an aggregrate multiplier. An advantage of multipliers derived from input-output tables is that they give separate values for each sector of the economy under analysis and the differential impact of the various sectors may be an important area of interest. In addition, the input-output approach generates a great deal of detailed data on the local economy which is of use not only in multiplier calculations. On the other hand there are substantial problems and costs in data collection and this is the main reason why such an approach has been used rarely in the U.K. For the Invergordon study, it was felt that the time available and the small size of the local economy would permit the collection of the necessary data and the construction of the input-output tables, and this was the approach chosen. The particular methodology is described below and the results are given in the subsequent chapters.

The basis of any input-output model is the transactions table which shows how the output of each industry is distributed among other industries and sectors of the economy. The table shows not only sales to final buyers (final demand) but also sales to all intermediate consumers, and thus presents a detailed account of the sales and purchases of each industry. The model is based on a series of assumptions, the main ones being those set out by Chenery and Clark:[1]

  (i) each commodity (or group of commodities) is supplied by a single industry or sector of production

 (ii) the inputs purchased by each sector are a function only of the level of output of that sector

(iii) the total effect of carrying on several types of production is the sum of the separate effects.

This third assumption rules out external economies and diseconomies.

The model used in the Invergordon study is an adaptation of the standard input-output model by Miernyk for a study of the impact of the space industry on the economy of Boulder, Colorado.[2] There is no need in this study to explain the mathematical formulation of the model and the interested reader is referred to Miernyk's study.

[1] H.B. Chenery and P.G. Clark: *Interindustry economics* (New York, 1959), pp. 33-34
[2] W.H. Miernyk: *Impact of the space program on a local economy* (Morgantown, 1967)

Regional input-output studies in the U.K.

Presumably mainly because of the lack of acceptable data at sub-national levels, regional studies have been rare in the U.K., unlike in the United States where data availability for individual states has encouraged a large number of regional and local studies. The first major attempt in the U.K. was the construction of an input-output table for the Welsh economy in 1960 by Nevin, Roe and Round[3]. This used 31 industry groups and identified two separate regions — Wales and the 'Rest of the U.K.' The main restrictive assumption used was that the technical interindustry relationships were the same for Wales as for the corresponding industries in the U.K. This assumption was dropped where detailed data for particular industries was available. Also, in the estimation of intermediate outputs it was assumed that all Welsh final demands were satisfied by the outputs of Welsh industries in all cases where those outputs were sufficiently large.

A similar approach, but on a much smaller scale, was used by Blake and McDowall in constructing a local input-output table for 1965 for the town of St. Andrews, with a population of around 10,000 and an economy dominated by tourism and the university.[4] National coefficients were used, except where local ones were demonstrably different, in which cases local surveys were undertaken.

The limitations of this approach have been generally recognised and attempts have been made, notably by Hewings in the U.K., to improve the accuracy of non-survey techniques in adapting national coefficients for local studies. These have involved the use of location quotients, relative supply-demand ratios etc. to derive tables for the West Midlands for 1954 and South-East Kent for 1963 and 1968, using the national tables for those years[5]. As with similar work in the United States, the use of non-survey techniques has not yielded generally acceptable results and since Hewing's work little progress along these lines has been made in the U.K.

In contrast, there have been three regional or local input-output studies based virtually entirely on survey data and the estimation therefore of true local coefficients: the study by Sadler and others of an aluminium smelter on the economy of Anglesey in 1969[6]; Morrison's study of the Peterborough economy in 1968[7]; and McNicoll's study of the Shetland economy in 1971[8]. The present study has obviously more in common with these three studies than the earlier ones.

The Anglesey study used 30 industrial sectors for an economy with a population of approximately 55,000 and adopted an interesting modification to the conventional model by incorporating a feedback sector relating the production matrix, via income created, with a further consumption matrix. The Peterborough study (population 100,000) was a straightforward application of the conventional model using 38 sectors,

[3] E. Nevin, A.R. Roe and J.I. Round: *The structure of the Welsh economy* (Cardiff, 1966)

[4] C. Blake and S. McDowall: *A local input-output table* in *Scottish Journal of Political Economy*, vol. 14 (1967)

[5] G.J.D. Hewings: *Regional input-output models in the U.K.* in *Regional Studies* vol. 5 (1971)

[6] P. Sadler, B. Archer and C. Owen: *Regional income multipliers* (Bangor, 1973)

[7] W.I. Morrison: *The development of an urban interindustry model,* three articles in each of parts 3 to 5 of *Environment and Planning,* vol. 5 (1973)

[8] I.H. McNicoll: *The Shetland economy* (Glasgow, 1976)

including households. It is interesting to note that only 12 of these sectors were manufacturing industries and the remainder services, with both the retail and local government sectors being disaggregated into seven separate sectors, the underlying rationale being that the main effects of exogenous changes in demand would be felt in the service sector. The results of most small area input-output studies certainly confirm this view. The Shetland study (population 18,000) was much smaller, using 16 sectors, including households, seven of which were manufacturing industries and the remainder services.

The construction of the model
At the outset of the study one of the major problems (which must confront any study of this type) was that of defining the area to be covered. In other words, it was necessary to identify the geographical area of impact of the aluminium smelter prior to the impact occurring. Various alternatives were tried but all were heavily constrained by the availability of published statistics. Initially, a wide area was divided into its constituent parishes and an attempt was made to define the region by grouping together those parishes which demonstrated similar values of certain functional variables - population and employment structure being the only ones available at this level of disaggregation. The analysis identified two fairly distinct regions, one of which differed only slightly from the area covered by the employ-ment offices of Invergordon and Dingwall.

This area as defined was used in the early stages of the study but the frequent problems of reconciling survey data with official published data — particularly on population — led to its abandonment in favour of the area covered exactly by the two employment offices, for which official employment data was available. Luckily, the differences were slight but in other instances this may well not have been the case. The area covered by the employment offices in practice formed the travel-to-work area for the towns of Invergordon and Dingwall and thus had some economic justifi-cation. The area excluded from the 'optimum' area was the south-eastern corner of Sutherland and, as is shown in Chapter 7, very few people from there travel daily to work at the smelter, although a significant number now do so for the oil-related developments.

In passing, it should be mentioned that an adjacent area to East Ross was also delineated — the area surrounding Inverness — and some data was collected for this area because of the strong links it has with East Ross. It was felt that there would be some advantages in an interregional model. In a single-region model exports are usually treated as exogenous, which does not eliminate the problem of their estimation but simply shifts the problem outside the model. If there are significant feedbacks this exogenous treatment is inadequate. In the case of a small region it is possible to neglect any feedbacks from the national economy but if the region has significant links with adjacent regions the lack of interregional data constitutes a serious handicap. It was expected that strong links between East Ross and Inverness would emerge and that it would be necessary to quantify these links but in the event they turned out to be relatively unimportant and did not justify the large-scale collection of data for the Inverness area. The main links were the use of Inverness whole-salers by firms and households in East Ross and the use of Inverness as a shopping centre but it was decided simply to aggregate such transactions with all other imports in the usual single-region model.

Another problem at the outset was the devision of a sectoring scheme. The standard transactions table has four main quadrants — the processing sector, the final demand sector, the payments sector and the quadrant showing the sales of primary factors to final demand. Because the purpose of the study was the analysis of the impact of the aluminium smelter on the local economy, attention was concentrated mainly on the processing sector and it was decided to leave the other quadrants as aggregated as possible. Thus only four final demand sectors were used — inventory accumulation, capital investment, households and exports — and the corresponding four payments sectors — inventory depletion, payments on capital account, households and imports. As was mentioned earlier, in the calculation of local multipliers the household row and column were incorporated in the processing sector. For many purposes such a high level of aggregation would be of little use but it was felt to be justified in the present study to allow resources to be concentrated on the collection of data for the processing sector.

The processing (or intermediate) sector was then divided into industry groups or sectors. This is a difficult task because ideally a sector should comprise establishments producing a homogenous product and this rarely occurs in practice. Data confidentiality and disclosure constraints are severe in small areas with very few firms and they tend to bring about a higher degree of aggregation than is normally desirable. In the Invergordon case the non-existence in the region of many manufacturing industries made the task relatively simple. After experimenting with a number of alternatives it was eventually decided to use eighteen industrial sectors, plus separate sectors for the construction of the smelter and its permanent operation, plus households. Table 5.1 lists these sectors together with their Minimum List Headings, according to the Standard Industrial Class-ification, which allows comparability with the sectoring schemes used for the U.K. tables. There are obvious problems with the aggregation of sectors with different technical production functions and differing spatial input requirements — e.g. with the 'other manufacturing' sector — but further disaggregation would have created additional problems. The number of processing sectors is less than those used in the Anglesey (30 sectors) and Peterborough (37 sectors) studies mentioned above but East Ross is a smaller area in terms of population. There are only five manu-facturing sectors (including the smelter) but in terms of the indirect effects on the local economy the service industries are certainly far more important, as the results below show. It is believed that the results of the impact assessment do not suggest that the level of disaggregation used was unsatisfactory, although the coefficients for individual industries must obviously be treated with caution.

The next task was the construction of the basic transactions matrix. Lists of firms, retail establishments etc. were compiled, largely from records provided by the Department of Employment and Ross and Cromarty County Council but also from telephone directories, newspapers etc. and these were updated regularly throughout the study. All establish-ments were classified by sector and the numbers in each group are shown in Table 5.1. Detailed information was collected for 1968 and 1972, although

Table 5.1 — Survey coverage

Industry	MLH	1968 No. establishments	1968 Employment	1968 Employment coverage	1972 No. establishments	1972 Employment	1972 Employment coverage
Agriculture	001	381	992	47.3	311	700	60.7
Forestry	002	4	63	100.0	5	101	100.0
Fishing	003	8	53	75.5	6	48	81.3
Mining and quarrying	102-103	3	33	100.0	3	29	100.0
Whisky distilling	239	8	320	92.8	8	361	93.9
Food processing	211-229	5	105	76.2	6	131	77.1
Mechanical engineering	331-349	4	80	100.0	6	69	100.0
All other manufacturing		14	302	96.0	21	505	95.6
Construction	500	23	1,254	71.9	29	1,382	57.8
Gas, electricity, water	601-603	4	293	100.0	4	318	100.0
Transport and communication	701-709	3	374	83.4	4	521	88.3
Distribution: wholesale	810-812	7	55	100.0	8	60	100.0
Distribution: retail	820-832	135	701	71.8	126	727	70.4
Insurance, banking	860-866	20	137	66.4	22	239	49.4
Professional services	871-879	42	969	67.7	47	1,094	64.2
Miscellaneous services	881-899	123	1,091	67.1	115	1,056	56.0
Local government	906	11	309	100.0	11	406	100.0
National government	901	2	94	100.0	2	145	100.0
Industry not stated			38			462*	100.0
Totals			7,263	73.1		8,612	72.0

* All British Aluminium employees

for many of the firms information was obtained for the whole study period. This was necessary in the cases of those firms whose financial years did not coincide with the calendar year (e.g. April to April). The main method of obtaining information was by way of a detailed questionnaire covering the nature and origin of sales and purchases, employment, capital investment, inventory changes etc. A standard questionnaire was devised with certain modifications for particular sectors (mainly the service industries) and on occasion individual firms and establishments.

In as many cases as possible interviews were arranged with firms and the information obtained directly in the course of the interviews, usually with parts of the questionnaire being filled in subsequently by the establishment concerned. An approach was made to every establishment in each sector with the exception of agriculture, retail distribution, professional and scientific services, and miscellaneous services, in which cases stratified random samples (using employment distributions) were taken, supplemented by a smaller postal questionnaire for the establishments not included in the samples. Table 5.1 gives the numbers of establishments in each sector, total employment, the numbers providing information and the proportion of employment covered by the respondents. It will be seen that for seven sectors coverage was 100% in both 1968 and 1972 and the overall coverage in the two years was 73% and 72% respectively (using employment as the measure). With the construction and operation of the smelter, the local government sector and parts of the construction and transport sectors access was given to the invoices/orders of the establishments concerned and the necessary information was obtained directly from these. This was a very lengthy task, particularly with regard to the County Council, but it provided a great deal of useful information not only on the sectors themselves but also indirectly on others.

It is certainly true that the response rate was very high by comparison with similar studies and justified the time spent on data collection. The advantages of East Ross in this regard were its small size and the widespread interest in the smelter and the study itself. Both the Highlands and Islands Development Board and the Ross and Cromarty Council had very close links with the business community and their support and involvement in the study was a great help in obtaining information. The vast data requirements of an input-output table constructed from survey work is, of course, the biggest disadvantage of such an approach and is the main reason why so few studies of this type have been undertaken in the U.K. In the Invergordon case, data collection alone took between two and three man years. It is therefore very difficult to generalize but it is encouraging to note that there are similarities in some of the results from the Anglesey, Shetland and Invergordon studies and it may be possible to devise some methods of reducing primary data requirements for any future studies in rural areas. This point is elaborated further in the concluding chapter.

Use was also made of 'control totals' to estimate gross output for each sector. These were intended primarily as a check on the direct survey results and also to 'gross up' the output of those sectors where coverage was not complete. A number of sources were used, varying according to the sector. In the first instance, figures for gross and net output per employee were obtained from the U.K. tables and then multiplied by the sector employment totals to give a rough indication of output for each sector.

Alternative estimates were obtained by multiplying the sector employment totals by the average output per employee figures obtained from the survey results for each sector. For some sectors a great deal of additional information was obtainable: for example, for the agricultural sector there is a wide range of published official data and the North of Scotland College of Agriculture regularly collect information on farm incomes in East Ross; and two extensive studies of agriculture in the region had been undertaken.[9]

---

[9] More detailed discussions are given in J. Ormiston: *Moray Firth: An agricultural study* (Inverness, 1973) and North of Scotland College of Agriculture: *An Agro-economic appraisal of agriculture in Easter Ross* (Aberdeen, 1967).

6 The construction phase

Although the main interest of the study was the impact of the permanent operation of the smelter, some attention was given to the construction phase which lasted from approximately March 1969 to October 1971. It is often forgotten that in rural areas the size and cost of large construction projects are frequently such that in some respects their implications are greater than those of the permanent facilities. For example, the Invergordon aluminium smelter cost around £40 million to build, compared with the annual local income injection of the production phase of around £1.25 million, and peak construction employment was 2,000, compared with the 700 permanent employees. This imbalance between the levels of construction activity and permanent operation generated certain effects which continued long after the construction phase was over.

Also, the construction phase provided the opportunity to test various techniques of analysis and sources of information for the study before the main work began. This proved very helpful. For both the construction and permanent phases the main technique used was regional input-output analysis and it was possible to iron out many of the problems in the earlier stages. The approach necessitated the construction of a set of accounts for the East Ross economy in 1968, the year prior to which construction work began. It was intended originally to collect the relevant data for each year since 1968 but this proved too big a task and detailed data was only collected subsequently for 1972, the year production began.

The input-output approach was chosen because of the detailed information it provided on all industries in the economy, including their structural interdependence, which allows the overall economic impact to be disaggregated into the impacts on individual industries and sectors. This is the main advantage of input-output analysis over the more common forms of regional multiplier analysis in the U.K., which are essentially highly aggregated. The main disadvantage is the vast amount of data collection required but in the case of the smelter it was felt that this approach would be necessary.

After collecting and analyzing the required data for 1968, the first step was to compile a table of interindustry transactions, showing the sales and purchases of the industrial sectors identified in the area, both among themselves and to final demand, exports, imports etc. The next step was to compute from the transactions table a matrix of technical (or input) coefficients, defined as the direct purchases by each industry from every other industry for each £ of output produced. This involved dividing each entry in each column of the processing sector in the transactions table by the total output of that column (adjusted to take account of stock changes etc.). Of course, these direct requirements do not represent the total input requirements: the agricultural industry, for example, may need to purchase 4p of inputs from the food processing industry to produce £1 of agricultural output, but to produce that extra 4p of output the food processing industry will have to purchase additional inputs from other industries (including, possibly, agricultural itself) . . . and there will consequently be a chain of indirect effects which have to be taken into account. Furthermore, one of the main inputs will be labour and the expenditure of wages and salaries earned in production will itself generate a chain of induced effects. In using input-output analysis to examine economic impact it is necessary therefore to take account of all the direct, indirect and induced effects and modern computer facilities make this possible.

Economic activity in East Ross was grouped into 18 industries, using the official standard industrial classification, and these are listed in Table 5.2. The basic transactions table for 1968 was built up from questionnaires and direct interviews and this was then used to generate the matrix of total input requirements, which is given as Table 6.1. This shows, for example, that for the agricultural industry to increase its final demand sales by one unit, it needs to purchase 0.006 units from the forestry industry, 0.003 units from the fishing industry, 0.006 units from mining and quarrying . . . and so on, reading down column 1. Purchases are entered in the columns and sales in the rows. It will be seen that the column total for agriculture is 1.641 which implies that if final demand sales are increased by £1, total output in the local economy would increase by £1.641 — which is equivalent to saying that the output multiplier for the agricultural industry is 1.641. In fact, output in the agricultural industry itself would increase by £1.091 because of the indirect and induced effects mentioned above.

The output multipliers will vary from industry to industry, according to their different input requirements, and particularly the volume of imports, but it is interesting to note from Table 6.1 that most of the values are in the range 1.25 to 1.75, which is in line with evidence from other comparable studies.[1]

Data was then obtained from British Aluminium and the contractors responsible for construction — Taywood Wrightson, a joint company established by Taylor Woodrow Construction (building, civil and mechanical engineers) and Head Wrightson (process plant engineers) — on the input requirements of the construction work and presented in a form comparable with that for other industries. This information is shown as the SC (smelter construction) row and column of Table 6.1. The column shows the estimated purchases made from local industries for each £ of output and, of course, there were no local sales.

Multiplying the SC column by the total construction cost gives the output column in Table 6.2 which shows the distribution of the increased output among the various local industries. In addition to the direct £40 million cost, it is estimated that local output increased by an additional £4.84 million, equivalent to an output multiplier of 1.121 — very low but understandable in light of the very high import content of machinery, equipment etc. As would be expected, the main local industries affected were agriculture (through the sale of land), mining and quarrying, construction and the service sector.

Again, it should be stressed that the figures in Table 6.2 are only estimates and are subject to the usual reservations surrounding input-output studies of this type. In particular, it is assumed that the input

---

[1] See, for example, P. Sadler: *Regional income multipliers* (Bangor, 1973)

Table 6.1 — 1968 Matrix of total input requirements

	1	2	3	4	5	6	7	8	9	10	11	12	13	14	15	16	17	18	SC
1	1.091	0.075	0.040	0.010	0.017	0.152	0.008	0.007	0.009	0.010	0.010	0.053	0.034	0.010	0.009	0.025	0.029	0.018	0.008
2	0.006	1.013	0.001	0.000	0.001	0.001	0.001	0.001	0.006	0.001	0.000	0.000	0.000	0.000	0.000	0.005	0.001	0.000	0.000
3	0.003	0.002	1.078	0.002	0.001	0.002	0.001	0.001	0.002	0.002	0.001	0.007	0.004	0.002	0.001	0.002	0.003	0.003	0.001
4	0.006	0.013	0.004	1.013	0.002	0.007	0.007	0.005	0.119	0.007	0.003	0.002	0.001	0.002	0.001	0.002	0.043	0.006	0.006
5	0.004	0.000	0.000	0.000	1.001	0.001	0.000	0.001	0.002	0.001	0.000	0.000	0.000	0.001	0.000	0.001	0.000	0.000	0.000
6	0.004	0.001	0.001	0.001	0.000	1.004	0.001	0.000	0.000	0.001	0.000	0.001	0.000	0.001	0.000	0.001	0.003	0.001	0.000
7	0.009	0.028	0.048	0.001	0.003	0.008	1.010	0.021	0.019	0.003	0.007	0.001	0.001	0.001	0.002	0.001	0.011	0.002	0.001
8	0.007	0.003	0.011	0.002	0.001	0.008	0.017	1.017	0.014	0.002	0.002	0.001	0.006	0.001	0.001	0.002	0.024	0.003	0.001
9	0.025	0.046	0.024	0.017	0.014	0.051	0.034	0.033	1.034	0.014	0.007	0.012	0.007	0.007	0.006	0.008	0.062	0.030	0.006
10	0.055	0.036	0.020	0.007	0.008	0.038	0.018	0.016	0.036	1.023	0.014	0.018	0.029	0.006	0.012	0.021	0.032	0.012	0.003
11	0.028	0.046	0.052	0.018	0.008	0.037	0.018	0.022	0.027	0.017	1.021	0.019	0.010	0.020	0.019	0.023	0.038	0.033	0.006
12	0.091	0.067	0.058	0.047	0.014	0.052	0.028	0.024	0.040	0.033	0.043	1.041	0.294	0.037	0.035	0.082	0.088	0.068	0.015
13	0.151	0.196	0.162	0.134	0.038	0.128	0.055	0.056	0.090	0.096	0.064	0.086	1.066	0.092	0.084	0.154	0.161	0.184	0.041
14	0.007	0.010	0.007	0.007	0.001	0.003	0.003	0.004	0.006	0.003	0.004	0.002	0.007	1.019	0.010	0.010	0.015	0.003	0.001
15	0.020	0.042	0.024	0.020	0.003	0.012	0.006	0.016	0.013	0.008	0.008	0.010	0.007	0.016	1.012	0.013	0.013	0.016	0.003
16	0.109	0.111	0.112	0.090	0.028	0.088	0.043	0.046	0.065	0.078	0.076	0.090	0.053	0.093	0.071	1.127	0.191	0.131	0.024
17	0.024	0.038	0.025	0.026	0.006	0.010	0.009	0.000	0.015	0.017	0.011	0.017	0.010	0.024	0.018	0.020	1.041	0.072	0.005
18	0.001	0.000	0.000	0.000	0.000	0.000	0.000	0.000	0.002	0.001	0.000	0.000	0.000	0.000	0.000	0.000	0.004	1.000	0.000
SC	0.000	0.000	0.000	0.000	0.000	0.000	0.000	0.000	0.000	0.000	0.000	0.000	0.000	0.000	0.000	0.000	0.000	0.000	1.000
T	1.641	1.727	1.667	1.395	1.146	1.620	1.260	1.279	1.499	1.317	1.271	1.350	1.529	1.331	1.282	1.491	1.763	1.583	1.121

Table 6.2 — Impact of the construction phase

		increases in output	increases in incomes	employment
1.	Agriculture	£320,000	£129,280	—
2.	Forestry	—	—	—
3.	Fishing	40,000	16,880	2
4.	Mining and quarrying	240,000	73,440	34
5.	Whisky distilling	—	—	—
6.	Food processing	—	—	—
7.	Mechanical engineering	40,000	8,200	9
8.	All other manufacturing	40,000	8,760	5
9.	Construction	240,000	60,480	27
10.	Gas, electricity and water	120,000	51,240	31
11.	Transport and communication	240,000	55,200	20
12.	Distribution: wholesale	600,000	205,800	65
13.	Distribution: retail	1,640,000	193,520	87
14.	Insurance, banking and finance	40,000	16,040	9
15.	Professional and scientific services	120,000	40,440	29
16.	Miscellaneous services	960,000	405,120	178
17.	Local government	200,000	97,000	71
18.	Other public admin. and defence	—	—	—
19.	Smelter construction	40,000,000	4,520,000	2,000
	Total	£44,840,000	£5,881,400	2,567

coefficients do not change during the period under consideration and, with construction lasting for some thirty months, it may well be that in some cases this assumption is invalid. This cautionary note applies also to the estimates of increases in personal incomes and employment arising from the output increases, which are based on the output:income rates prevailing in 1968 and the incremental output:employment ratios for the period 1968-72, the incremental ratios should have been used for both incomes and employment but this proved impossible in the former case. In any case, the margins of error are reduced in the present situation because the direct effects are far greater than the induced and indirect effects. Of the estimated £5.9 million increase in personal incomes, £4.5 million was attributable to the wages and salaries of those employed on the construction of the smelter. Similarly, of the estimated 2,567 jobs 2,000 of these were direct employees on the site. Nevertheless, bearing in mind all these qualifications, it is believed that Table 6.2 provides a reasonable picture of the impact of the construction phase on the East Ross economy.

Given that the main local effects were transmitted through the labour market, it was felt that it would be worth looking at this aspect in more detail, particularly in terms of the numbers employed and their origins. Table 6.3 sets out the numbers employed each month (based on counts undertaken at the beginning of each month). The numbers are of hourly-paid employees only and exclude the managerial, administrative and clerical staff, of whom there were just under 200 at the peak period. Figures have been given separately for the major firms and contracts.

The scale and timing of employment was very important. The peak of 2,000 employees compares with the total employment of around 7,300 in the summer of 1968. It can be seen from Table 6.3 that this peak was reached slowly but that from early 1971 employment fell sharply. This pattern was reflected in the local unemployment situation, the percentage figures for which are shown in Table 6.4. Earlier, it was pointed out that the high level of unemployment in East Ross was one of the main reasons behind the efforts to attract industry to the area and certainly the numbers fell significantly when construction work began at the smelter but, as the table shows, there was a marked deterioration when construction activity began to run down and from March 1971 onwards the numbers unemployed were higher than for many years.

Two main factors underlay this phenomenon: firstly, the deterioration in the national economy, which led inter alia to the liquidation of Duncan Logan Construction Ltd. (the largest construction firm in the area) and, secondly, the fact that many of the construction workers who had moved into East Ross decided to stay, probably in anticipation of work beginning on the proposed Grampian Chemicals' petrochemical plant, which in the event did not materialize. Luckily, Highlands Fabricators' choice of Nigg as a suitable site for building steel production platforms alleviated the unemployment problem when it was rapidly approaching a critical state but this should not be allowed to disguise the short-term consequences of large construction projects in rural areas. It is a serious problem which may well occur elsewhere, with more lasting consequences.

In comparison with similar projects, a surprisingly high number of local people sought and secured employment on the site. The definition of "local residents" was taken to be those who had resided in the area during the two years prior to the incoming of British Aluminium. Although this was rather arbitrary it had the advantage of distinguishing separately those who had previously left East Ross and returned at the advent of employment. The evidence does suggest that the proportion of local people employed on the site was noticeably higher than comparable sites elsewhere and that many local people were able to secure (relatively) stable employment, albeit generally of an unskilled or semi-skilled nature. The reasons commonly put forward for this high proportion of local people is the isolation of the Invergordon site from areas with developments of comparable size and the

**Table 6.3 Employment in construction work
(excluding administrative and clerical staff etc.)**

	Taylor Woodrow	Head Wrightson	Other site contracts	Housing contract	Pier contract	Total
March 1969	181		42	78		301
April	225		102	81		408
May	275		45	59		379
June	336		58	71	21	486
July	371		58	70	34	533
August	471		32	70	38	611
September	536	3	28	91	50	708
October	560	4	46	92	70	772
November	581	7	61	96	70	815
December	575	16	106	107	68	872
January 1970	563	34	118	116	71	902
February	558	31	142	140	62	933
March	527	52	176	122	61	938
April	589	79	174	115	58	1,015
May	655	185	335	109	56	1,340
June	700	216	413	118	53	1,500
July	739	302	489	182	65	1,777
August	770	291	448	181	59	1,749
September	752	309	489	169	48	1,767
October	715	327	434	105	32	1,613
November	662	369	446	136	16	1,629
December	612	386	437	127	6	1,568
January 1971	593	316	363	116	5	1,393
February	558	266	382	116	4	1,326
March	542	269	404	132	—	1,347
April	515	248	386	146	—	1,295
May	365	223	362	117	—	950
June	328	178	329	114	—	835
July	243	157	142	68	—	610
August	88	62	133	70	—	345
September	57	12	49	69	—	187
October	6	—	26	56	—	88

adequate pool of local labour during the construction phase. The expansion and contraction of employment affected non-locals most, with noticeable fluctuations in the numbers commuting daily into the area, e.g. from Inverness, and living in the construction camp located adjacent to the site. For example, the numbers living in the camp increased from 87 in August 1969 to 526 in August 1970 and fell to 100 in June 1971. Of the total construction labour force in August 1969, 65% could be regarded as locals; in August 1970 40%; and in June 1971 70%.

As regards the effects on other firms and industries in the area, some benefited substantially from the increased activity, as shown by Table 6.2, both directly as suppliers to the contractors and indirectly through the increased spending in the shops, pubs etc. The main adverse effects were obviously labour losses and to try to provide some reasonable information on these, data was obtained from periodic surveys of the personnel records of the site contractors. Information for two dates on the industrial origins (i.e. previous employment by industry) is given in Table 6.5, which distinguishes between locals and non-locals. It will be seen that the main sources of local labour were the construction, agricultural, transport and communications industries, the distributive trades, certain services and the unemployed. Many subcontractors brought specialized labour with them as, for example, is demonstrated by non-local recruitment from the engineering industries. Really, only a few points need to be made to support the data in the table. Firstly, the amalgamation of farm holdings and the continuing modernization of agriculture meant that during the period under consideration agricultural labour was being released and many of those who left to work on the construction site were not replaced. Agricultural labour in the East Ross area fell by an average of 6.5% per annum during the years 1968-1971. Secondly, there was substantial surplus labour in the distributive trades and this sector was also in a position to release labour. Thirdly, a number of other firms in the area were undergoing reorganization — even liquidation (e.g. the Duncan Logan companies) — and releasing labour. The general situation was therefore one of an adequate supply of labour sufficiently skilled to adapt to work on a large construction site and Taywood Wrightson and the main subcontractors found little difficulty in recruiting labour while most sectors of the local economy suffered few unwanted losses.

Nevertheless certain sectors experienced turnover and recruitment problems and to try to identify these sectors in more detail a postal questionnaire was sent to most employers in the area. Personal approaches were made to all firms and establishments employing more than 20 people. The purpose of the questionnaire was to obtain information on effects on turnover, recruitment and wage rates. Most of the major employers provided detailed and invaluable information and the returns generally give support to the points made above about the negligible effects on most firms. Firms which did report significant losses said that they were able to find replacements with little difficulty — usually from farms and the local authorities, in some cases from outside the area and from the pool of unemployed. Increases in wage rates were mainly attributed to national agreements and not changes in local labour market conditions and many firms apparently unable to offer wage rates comparable with those on site overcame their difficulties by improving fringe benefits and overtime earnings. A strong impression given is that many local firms — both small and large — have built up loyal, often long-serving staffs whose motivations were very largely unresponsive to the advantages of employment on the construction site.

Table 6.4 — Percentage unemployment figures, 1968-72

	1968	1969	1970	1971	1972
A. MALES					
January	13.0	10.5	9.6	10.3	14.7
February	11.1	8.9	8.2	10.4	14.3
March	9.8	7.6	7.4	10.3	12.6
April	9.2	6.6	6.1	10.2	10.1
May	7.9	5.3	5.0	10.2	7.9
June	7.4	4.4	4.8	11.1	5.7
July	5.8	5.9	4.6	12.9	4.6
August	7.3	6.3	4.8	14.4	4.7
September	7.5	6.2	5.0	14.7	5.1
October	8.5	6.5	6.2	15.2	4.7
November	9.2	6.4	6.9	16.0	4.8
December	9.0	7.3	8.6	14.1	4.5
B. TOTAL					
January	11.0	9.5	8.4	8.6	12.9
February	9.5	8.6	7.4	8.4	12.6
March	8.3	7.5	6.9	8.4	11.3
April	7.8	6.4	5.4	8.3	9.4
May	6.4	5.1	4.5	7.7	7.4
June	5.9	4.2	4.1	8.4	5.5
July	6.0	5.5	3.9	9.8	4.7
August	5.9	5.6	4.1	10.9	4.8
September	6.0	5.5	4.4	11.3	5.0
October	7.0	5.9	5.3	11.8	4.6
November	8.1	6.1	6.1	13.1	5.2
December	8.2	6.8	7.4	12.3	5.1

Source: Department of Employment

Table 6.5 — Industrial origins of construction workers

	Industry	Locals		Non-locals	
		Feb. 1970	Feb. 1971	Feb. 1970	Feb. 1971
I	Agriculture, Forestry, Fishing	49	61	1	4
II	Mining and quarrying	9	12	5	13
III	Food, drink and tobacco	17	21	1	6
IV	Coal and petroleum products	—	—	6	17
V	Chemicals and allied industries	3	3	2	9
VI	Metal Manufacture	1	3	2	12
VII	Mechanical engineering	25	28	40	84
VIII	Instrument Engineering	—	—	6	29
IX	Electrical Engineering	—	—	4	32
X	Shipbuilding and Marine Engineering	4	6	21	44
XI	Vehicles	—	—	11	22
XII	Metal Goods not elsewhere specified	—	—	—	—
XIII	Textiles	—	—	—	6
XIV	Leather, leather goods and fur	—	—	—	—
XV	Clothing and Footwear	—	—	1	—
XVI	Bricks, pottery, glass, cement, etc.	10	13	2	2
XVII	Timber, furniture, etc.	6	3	—	1
XVIII	Paper, printing and publishing	—	—	1	4
XIX	Other Manufacturing Industries	—	4	4	11
XX	Contruction	72	83	108	232
XXI	Gas, Electricity and water	18	26	3	11
XXII	Transport and Communication	42	50	3	19
XXIII	Distributive Trades	35	41	—	10
XXIV	Insurance, Banking, Finance and Business Services	6	6	—	2
XXV	Professional and Scientific Services	9	7	2	5
XXVI	Miscellaneous Services	20	44	11	38
XXVII	Public Administration and Defence Industry not stated	36	42	2	11
	Unemployed	63	86	33	56
	TOTAL	425	539	269	680

7 The permanent phase

Although in terms of employment and income generation the effects of the construction phase were far greater than those of the smelter's permanent operation, it was the latter which was of greater interest and in many respects the construction phase was used to test certain approaches and techniques of analysis with a view to their use in examining the effects of the operating phase.

As was discussed in Chapter 3, the Invergordon smelter was of a very modern design and more capital-intensive than the Anglesey and Lynemouth smelters which were constructed at the same time. It was inevitable, therefore, that some skilled labour would have to be brought in to run the plant and that sophisticated training programmes would be required for local people recruited. It would certainly be true to say that British Aluminium set out with a strong intention to integrate their operations with the local community as well as possible, including a stated objective to employ as many local people as possible. Of course, this is a common promise of firms wishing to build new plants in areas where there is likely to be opposition but it is one which in practice is rarely fulfilled. In the Invergordon case it is possible to compare intentions with achievements (and this is done below) but it should be said that British Aluminium started with some advantages, largely derived from their long-standing operation of their other Highland smelters and the existence at senior management level of employees who had either been brought up or had lived in the Highlands. Indeed, this was one of the reasons for the choice of Invergordon for the new smelter.

Local multipliers

In assessing the overall impact of the smelter on the local economy, the input-output approach was again used. The impact of the construction phase was analyzed using the 1968 transactions table for the East Ross area and condensing the construction activity into one calendar year. For the operational phase, a similar transactions table for 1972 was constructed, using the same 18 industrial sectors (as listed in Table 5.2) and based on data collected virtually entirely from surveys of firms and organizations in the area. From the transactions table, the matrix of input coefficients was computed and this is shown as Table 7.1. A comparison of this table with the 1968 input coefficients matrix (Table 6.1) shows some significant changes in input patterns, particularly for the service industries, but these are largely as would be expected in view of the developments in the local economy since 1968. Also, in small economies such as East Ross, the volume and nature of imports often change substantially over short periods of time, with consequent implications for local purchasing patterns.

The operation of the smelter is shown as the BA row and column of Table 7.1 which set out the local purchases and sales in 1972, the first normal year of production (although output was not at full capacity). As would be expected, the main local impact is by way of employment (and the consumption expenditure of employees) and the direct purchases from

Table 7.1 — 1972 Matrix of total input requirements

	1	2	3	4	5	6	7	8	9	10	11	12	13	14	15	16	17	18	BA
1	1.006	0.023	0.013	0.005	0.007	0.050	0.003	0.004	0.005	0.007	0.004	0.006	0.017	0.005	0.005	0.008	0.009	0.002	0.003
2	0.003	1.013	0.000	0.000	0.000	0.000	0.000	0.000	0.001	0.000	0.000	0.000	0.000	0.000	0.000	0.000	0.000	0.000	0.000
3	0.001	0.001	1.011	0.000	0.000	0.020	0.000	0.000	0.001	0.000	0.000	0.001	0.001	0.001	0.001	0.001	0.001	0.000	0.000
4	0.004	0.006	0.002	1.003	0.002	0.003	0.004	0.002	0.092	0.003	0.001	0.001	0.001	0.001	0.001	0.001	0.014	0.001	0.001
5	0.002	0.000	0.000	0.090	1.009	0.000	0.000	0.002	0.000	0.000	0.000	0.000	0.000	0.000	0.000	0.000	0.000	0.000	0.000
6	0.000	0.000	0.000	0.000	0.000	1.001	0.000	0.000	0.000	0.000	0.000	0.000	0.000	0.000	0.000	0.000	0.000	0.000	0.000
7	0.005	0.021	0.024	0.000	0.000	0.004	1.003	0.009	0.008	0.000	0.003	0.000	0.000	0.000	0.000	0.000	0.004	0.001	0.001
8	0.005	0.001	0.016	0.001	0.003	0.007	0.010	1.024	0.011	0.000	0.002	0.000	0.000	0.000	0.000	0.000	0.011	0.002	0.003
9	0.014	0.028	0.015	0.030	0.017	0.033	0.016	0.021	1.014	0.015	0.005	0.009	0.005	0.004	0.004	0.010	0.033	0.008	0.005
10	0.062	0.026	0.018	0.013	0.009	0.034	0.020	0.016	0.027	1.009	0.010	0.015	0.024	0.010	0.010	0.015	0.024	0.005	0.027
11	0.023	0.043	0.048	0.027	0.009	0.030	0.019	0.023	0.015	0.011	1.016	0.014	0.009	0.014	0.011	0.014	0.024	0.006	0.011
12	0.088	0.051	0.057	0.049	0.016	0.054	0.034	0.027	0.042	0.034	0.032	1.044	0.343	0.037	0.034	0.093	0.091	0.024	0.024
13	0.139	0.123	0.138	0.116	0.040	0.115	0.062	0.056	0.070	0.084	0.070	0.076	1.064	0.100	0.088	0.140	0.160	0.051	0.058
14	0.006	0.005	0.008	0.004	0.001	0.004	0.002	0.003	0.006	0.001	0.001	0.001	0.008	1.016	0.005	0.008	0.011	0.002	0.001
15	0.021	0.046	0.028	0.013	0.008	0.013	0.004	0.008	0.005	0.005	0.009	0.004	0.008	0.017	1.012	0.015	0.020	0.009	0.005
16	0.108	0.105	0.131	0.097	0.037	0.089	0.051	0.051	0.059	0.077	0.096	0.091	0.064	0.093	0.085	1.118	0.172	0.051	0.056
17	0.025	0.034	0.028	0.034	0.009	0.033	0.016	0.012	0.017	0.018	0.016	0.015	0.012	0.020	0.020	0.024	1.024	0.025	0.049
18	0.000	0.000	0.000	0.000	0.000	0.000	0.000	0.000	0.000	0.000	0.000	0.000	0.000	0.000	0.000	0.000	0.001	1.000	0.000
BA	0.000	0.000	0.000	0.000	0.000	0.000	0.000	0.000	0.000	0.000	0.000	0.000	0.000	0.000	0.000	0.00	0.000	0.000	1.000
T	1.572	1.526	1.537	1.392	1.167	1.490	1.244	1.255	1.372	1.266	1.265	1.276	1.556	1.318	1.276	1.447	1.604	1.187	1.244

local firms are very small. Also, there are no local sales, with the entire output of aluminium being exported from the area to B.A. processing plants elsewhere in Scotland and the rest of the U.K.

Table 7.2 sets out the distribution of increased output among the various industries comprising the local economy. Three categories have been identified — direct, indirect and induced — and it can be seen that, apart from the smelter's gross output of £4,152,000, the increases are small.. Direct purchases from local industries amounted to only £315,552, most of which accrued to the local authority in payment of rates and to the public utilities, including transport. Furthermore, the indirect increase in local output was only £49,824, demonstrating the lack of significant inter-industry linkages in the East Ross economy. In contrast the induced increase, arising from the consumption expenditures of direct and indirect employees, was relatively large, at £647,712. Overall, the main local industries benefiting were retail distribution, miscellaneous services, local government, public utilities (gas, electricity, water), wholesale distribution and transport.

The total increase in local output and its distribution among local industries, as shown in the final column of Table 7.2, is obtained by multiplying the B.A. column of Table 7.1 by the gross direct output of the smelter. In 1972 the total increase in local output was estimated to be approximately £5,165,088 which, in relation to the B.A. output of £4,152,000, is equivalent to an output multiplier of 1.24. This is higher than the output multiplier of the construction phase (1.12) but still relatively low because of the absence of local sales of aluminium and because the major raw materials were imported.

The increase in local output is also shown in Table 7.3, along with the increases in personal incomes and employment. The other figures were derived from the output data in the same way as used for the construction phase: using the output:income ratios for the various industries in 1972 and the incremental output:employment ratios identified for the period 1968-72. As with the analysis of the smelter's construction, the incremental ratios should have been used for both incomes and employment but this was impossible in the former case. The estimated total increase in personal incomes in 1972 was £1,225,158, including the smelter's wage bill of £892,680, which implies a local income multiplier of 1.37. Of the estimated total increase in local employment of 733, 550 were the smelter's employees, implying a local employment multiplier of 1.33. As with the changes in output, most of the increases in incomes and employment were in the service sector.

The various multipliers generated by this input-output approach, there-fore, are all small: output 1.24, incomes 1.37 and employment 1.33. The low values, however, are not inconsistent with earlier work on regional multipliers in the U.K.

Since the late 1960s there has been growing interest in regional multipliers and a number of empirical studies have been published. In 1967 Archibald[1], by calculating the likely magnitude of the leakages from the multiplier process, estimated that income multipliers for the standard

---

[1] G.C. Archibald: *Regional multiplier effects in the U.K.* in *Oxford Economic Papers* (1967)

Table 7.2 — Distribution of increased output

	direct	indirect	induced	total
1. Agriculture	—	—	£12,456	£12,456
2. Forestry	—	—	—	—
3. Fishing	—	—	—	—
4. Mining and quarrying	—	£4,152	—	4,152
5. Whisky distilling	—	—	—	—
6. Food processing	—	—	—	—
7. Mechanical engineering	£4,152	—	—	4,152
8. All other manufacturing	8,304	4.152	—	12,456
9. Construction	4,152	4,152	12,456	20,760
10. Gas, electricity and water	95,496	4,152	12,456	112,104
11. Transport and communication	16,608	4,152	24,912	45,672
12. Distribution wholesale	4,152	8,304	87,192	99,648
13. Distribution retail	—	4,152	236,664	240,816
14. Insurance, banking and finance	—	—	4,152	4,152
15. Professional and scientific services	4,152	4,152	12,456	20,760
16. Miscellaneous services	12,456	12,456	207,600	232,512
17. Local government	166,080	—	37,368	203,448
18. Other public admin. and defence	—	—	—	—
19. British Aluminium	4,152,000	—	—	4,152,000
Total	£4,467,552	£49,824	£647,712	£5,165,088

planning regions of the U.K. would normally be in the range 1.2 to 1.7. Brown[2] produced estimates at the bottom end of that range — 1.28 for the Development Areas as a whole and 1.24 for smaller regions. Allen[3] estimated that the income multiplier for Scotland would be between 1.4 and 1.5 and Steel[4] produced estimates for individual regions ranging from 1.19 for Yorkshire and Humberside to 1.41 for South East England, with significantly higher values of 1.70 or 1.89 for Scotland (due to the low savings and import coefficients).

There is undoubtedly some relationship between the size of a region and the value of the multiplier[5] and it is often assumed that the smaller the region, the lower the value of the multiplier. This is not necessarily so because the crucial factor is the volume of leakages from the local economy but it is usually the case that in small areas the economic base is so small and specialized that imports are very high and the multiplier correspondingly low. Most empirical studies in the U.K. (and, indeed, elsewhere) bear this out. Czamanski, for example, concluded that "the low multiplier effects characteristic of the Nova Scotia economy result from high import components in most sectors of the local economy."[6]

A priori, therefore, multiplier values for the Invergordon smelter lower than the estimates for Scotland and the English regions would have been expected. There have been a few studies in the U.K. of the impacts of industrial developments in rural areas which offer some useful comparisons with the Invergordon experience. The obvious one is the study by Sadler and others of the Anglesey aluminium smelter[7], for which the estimated income multipliers were 1.50 for the operational phase and 1.26 for the construction phase. This study also used an input-output model and the income multipliers estimated for other industries ranged from 1.007 for rail transport to 1.759 for agriculture, reasonably consistent with the Invergordon results. Greig's study of the impact of the Fort William pulp and paper mill[8] produced income multipliers in the range 1.44 - 1.54 and employment multipliers of 1.90 - 2.65 but this was an unusual development in that the main input, timber, was obtained locally and therefore local interindustry linkages were very important. Greig's more recent work on the impact of the H.I.D.B.'s fisheries programmes[9] also produced relatively high multiplier values for the fishery industry: for the four sub-regions of Argyll, Orkney and Mainland, Outer Isles, and Shetland the income multipliers were 1.37, 1.39, 1.43 and 1.41 and the employment multipliers 1.53, 1.91, 1.65 and 2.83 respectively. Again, in these cases the backward and forward linkages into boatbuilding and fish processing were very strong, particularly in Shetland, and would account for the high values.

[2] A.J. Brown and others: *The Green Paper on Development Areas* in *National Institute economic review* (1967)

[3] K.J. Allen: *The regional multiplier* in S.C. Orr and J.B. Cullingworth (eds): *Regional and urban studies* (London, 1969)

[4] D.B. Steele: *Regional multipliers in Great Britain* in *Oxford Economic Papers* (1969)

[5] See G.C. Archibald, op. cit.

[6] S. Czamanski: *Regional science techniques in practice* (Lexington, 1972), p.222

[7] P.G. Sadler and others: *Regional income multipliers* (Bangor, 1973)

[8] M.A. Greig: *The regional income and employment effects of a paper mill* in *Scottish Journal of Political Economy* (1971)

[9] M.A. Greig: *The economic impact of the H.I.D.B. investment in fisheries* (Inverness, 1972)

Table 7.3 — Annual impact of the operational phase

| | | increases in | | |
		output	incomes	employ- ment
1.	Agriculture	£12,456	£4,758	—
2.	Forestry	—	—	—
3.	Fishing	—	—	—
4.	Mining and quarrying	4,152	1,042	1
5.	Whisky distilling	—	—	—
6.	Food processing	—	—	—
7.	Mechanical engineering	4,152	934	1
8.	All other manufacturing	12,456	2,516	1
9.	Construction	20,760	4,546	2
10.	Gas, electricity and water	112,104	40,133	29
11.	Transport and communication	45,672	11,966	3
12.	Distribution wholesale	99,648	29,994	11
13.	Distribution retail	240,816	32,510	13
14.	Insurance, banking and finance	4,152	1,702	1
15.	Professional and scientific services	20,760	7,183	5
16.	Miscellaneous services	232,512	91,842	43
17.	Local government	203,448	103,352	73
18.	Other public admin. and defence	—	—	—
19.	British Aluminium	4,152,000	892,680	550
	Total	£5,165,088	£1,225,158	733

Also, Greig used a neo-Keynesian multiplier approach which is bound to generate values slightly different from those using input-output analysis.

Overall, the Invergordon results are compatible with earlier work in the U.K. As Table 7.2 clearly shows the indirect effects of the smelter's operation are very small, because of the lack of important interindustry linkages in the East Ross economy and the smelter's reliance on imported inputs, and the induced effects arising from consumption expenditure are significantly greater. The implications of this pattern for future policies in the area are discussed in the concluding section of this report.

Finally, it is worth considering whether or not the multiplier results, based on 1972 data, are likely to be typical of the smelter's continuing operations. This is difficult to assess, not least because of the qualifications regarding the original data and the results themselves. Van Duijn[10] has shown that theoretically the value of the multiplier is very likely to change over time and Bourque's study of the Washington economy[11] stressed the importance of cyclical fluctuations in small regional economies. The latter calculated income multipliers for 27 industrial sectors and over the period 1963-67 the values of 24 of the 27 multipliers fell. The average value of the multiplier declined from 1.20 to 1.05. Sadler also has suggested that if incomes in an area rise, the demand for locally produced goods may fall as people change to different (usually more expensive consumption patterns).[12] On the other hand, there are time-lags associated with new developments and with changes in the components of expenditure and, for example, "some time may elapse before firms become aware of a rise in their sales and probably more time before they feel satisfied that the rise is likely to be sufficiently sustained to justify an increase in production."[13] This has certainly been the case in the Invergordon area with the retail sector, where recently new supermarkets and other shops have been established, after some delay.

Unfortunately, the advent of oil-related developments to the area — principally the Highlands Fabricators' platform yard which began work in 1972 and currently employs around 2,300 people (although in 1974 the labour force reached a peak of 3,300) and the MK-Shand pipecoating yard which also began operations in 1972 and currently employs around 750 — has made it impossible to ascertain which new developments are a consequence of the aluminium smelter or the other activities.

The direct impact of the smelter has certainly increased since 1972. In particular, the labour force has risen to just over 700, partly as a result of the great pressure on the local labour market from the oil-related firms, and the 1976 wage bill was just over £2 million compared with £890,000 in 1972. Similarly, rate payments to the local authority have more than doubled and there have been comparable increases in other local payments. The total direct increase in output in 1976 was probably around £9 million, compared with £4 million in 1972.

There have been no major changes in input patterns, however, nor the

---

[10] J.J. Van Duijn: *An interregional model of economic fluctuations* (Farnborough, 1972)
[11] P.J. Bourque: *An input-output analysis of economic change in Washington State* in *University of Washington Business Review* (1971)
[12] P. Sadler and others, op. cit.
[13] T. Wilson: *The regional multiplier: a critique* in *Oxford Economic Papers* (1968)

establishment in the area of firms using aluminium as an input. Without the latter or an alumina plant, the indirect effects will continue to be very small. The induced effects will have risen as a result of the increased incomes of British Aluminium employees and there are clear signs that the value of the multiplier will have increased because of changes in consumption patterns, as mirrored by the improvements in retail provision in the area. At the time of the smelter's establishment there was a good deal of excess capacity in the local service sector, a consequence of the area's history of emigration, but in the course of recent population growth a number of thresholds have been reached, necessitating additional service facilities such as shops, schools etc. It seems likely that the income and employment multiplier values for the Invergordon smelter are now in the range 1.40 to 1.45 and these could be regarded as the stable values.

8 Labour market impact

73% of the total increase in incomes and 75% of the increase in employment was attributable to B.A.'s own employees. The local labour market aspects, therefore, merited detailed attention and a great deal of information was obtained from B.A. on their labour force, the main aspects of which are summarized below.

Whilst construction was underway, one of the main tasks was the recruitment of the permanent labour force. In 1968 a nucleus of about 30 staff, headed by the plant manager-designate (Gordon Drummond), was set up in London. Their work consisted mainly of a detailed evaluation of existing smelters, including the Reynolds plants in North America, and the choice and evaluation of the engineering design for Invergordon. The plant is in fact the most capital-intensive smelter in the world. Considerations of labour supply were irrelevant to the choice of technique of production and the structure of labour demand was determined subsequently. The small nucleus produced detailed manpower schedules showing requirements over time and a recruitment philosophy was established. Basically, the smelter is organized in seven departments:

1. Management
2. Accounting
3. Engineering
4. Industrial engineering
5. Personnel
6. Production (a) carbon
   (b) casting
   (c) reduction
7. Technical

The employment level of 700 is significantly above the original estimate of 550 (which was the average level during 1972 and which was used in the earlier tables). There were a number of reasons for this revision of manpower requirements. In part the revision was a consequence of the delay in reaching full production resulting from the downturn in the world aluminium market. This delay coincided with a substantial change in local labour market conditions as Highlands Fabricators and other oil-related companies moved into East Ross. For British Aluminium this obviously altered their ability to continue the planned manpower build-up and find replacements for any leavers, and a partial solution was to increase manning levels. Also, in certain sections of the plant the company underestimated manpower requirements. Three fairly common views on this were expressed in the series of interviews held with employees: the first was the feeling that the original manpower schedules were based too much on experience and practices in the United States; the second was that the company had overestimated the productive capacities of locally recruited employees; and the third was that the trade unions had exerted strong pressures to increase the size of the labour force. None of these views was completely accepted by the management staff interviewed but there are certainly elements of truth in all three. The outstanding revision in the manpower schedules concerned the number of craftsmen required: the original estimate was 50 while the present requirement is 120. Day-only maintenance proved insufficient and craftsmen now work the shift system.

Once the detailed requirements were known, the next stage was recruitment. There were five principal sources of candidates for employment:

(i) the transfer of existing employees from the Company's other plants

(ii) unsolicited external advertizing

(iii) from registers of people seeking employment maintained, for example, by the Department of Employment and the Highlands and Islands Development Board (the "Counterdrift" register)

(iv) external advertizing

(v) "head hunting", i.e. the practice of approaching and recruiting specific people already in employment.

Different sources were used for the different vacancies to be filled. In terms of the biggest group to be recruited, the hourly rated, the common procedure was to advertize (exclusively) in the local press. This advertizing was of both a general and specific nature. In cases where the Personnel Department felt that local potential was inadequate — e.g. as regards craftsmen — advertizements were placed in the Aberdeen and Glasgow papers and occasionally outwith Scotland in other heavily industrialized areas — e.g. South Wales, North East England, the Midlands etc. This geographical distribution of advertizing in part explains the geographical distribution of applications for employment.

Local interest in the plant, however, was widespread as a consequence, inter alia, of the planning inquiries, local elections and the construction work. There was therefore a large number of unsolicited applications, both from locals and from elsewhere. In the first instance the local response to the press advertizing was disappointing. The B.A. management felt that this was because local people had been overimpressed by the development and probably felt that they would not be good enough to be employed. The company's answer was to undertake a series of public meetings in the area and within a few weeks this publicity had generated about 250 local applicants.

Regarding the recruitment of hourly rated employees, the company instituted a special arrangement with the local office of the Department of Employment by which the Department acted as a filter. In the first instance all applications for hourly rated employment went to them and on the basis of general guidelines provided by British Aluminium the Department of Employment selected the most suitable applicants. The general guidelines related to a stable job record, residence within ten miles of the plant, suitable age and a willingness to work shifts. In the event, the Department of Employment recommended to the Personnel Department about one third of all applicants; these were offered interview by the company; and approximately one third of those interviewed were appointed. A broad generalization would therefore be that of every nine applicants, three were interviewed and one appointed.

The interview sessions were vitually whole-day sessions with five elements:

(i) an introductory session during which the applicant's application form was discussed

(ii) an industrial relations interview during which the company's "Agreement" was explained

(iii) an aptitude test, including a written trade test

(iv) a medical examination

 (v) a selection interview with a superior.

About sixteen people per day went through these interview sessions and in the evening there was a internal B.A. meeting, attended by those directly involved in the sessions and others involved in recruitment, at which decisions were made to appoint or reject.

Less formal arrangements were made for the interviewing and appointment of salaried and clerical staff. In some instances the interviews were held elsewhere — e.g. in Glasgow — and suitable candidates were subsequently invited to bring their wives to East Ross on an introductory visit. In most of these cases the company were looking for people with particular and specified skills and hence the interviewing procedures were much more straightforward.

A detailed analysis was undertaken of personal data relating to those who were employed by the company. This data concerned age, sex, family size, place of birth, previous residence, previous employment history etc. Most of this information was taken from the original application forms of employees which were made available (in confidence) by British Aluminium. Where application forms were incomplete, gaps in the information sought were filled as far as possible from the personal knowledge of the Personnel Department.

The extraction of data was undertaken in fact in two stages. The exercise was first done in August 1971 when the number of employees totalled 404 — this corresponded roughly with what can be called the first stage of recruitment. The exercise was repeated in July 1973 when the number of employees had increased to 669. Of the original 404 employees, 287 were still with the company. It was therefore possible to identify four groups of employees: all employees at July 1973 (669); all employees at August 1971 (404); all second phase employees (382); and all first phase 'continuees' (287). In addition, two other groups of interest could be identified: those who had been employed by British Aluminium and had left; and the unsuccessful applicants.

For each of the variables below data was collected and analyzed for these six groups. The tables for all employees at July 1973 are presented in the main text of this chapter, as are some of those for the unsuccessful applicants; those relating to employees who had left are summarized below.

British Aluminium's labour force at July 1973 can be broken down thus:

	male	female	total
Hourly rated	422	4	426
Clerical and others	60	25	85
Salaried	147	11	158
	629	40	669

Tables 8.1A and 8.1B set out the age and sex distributions of the 669 employees. It will be immediately obvious that virtually all of these are

63

Table 8.1A — All employees at July 1973. Age and sex distribution

Age group	Hourly Rated		Clerical		Salaried		Total		
	male	female	male	female	male	female	male	female	total
15 - 19	4	—	14	5	—	1	18	6	24
20 - 24	75	—	13	9	11	2	99	11	110
25 - 29	95	—	9	4	29	3	133	7	140
30 - 34	79	—	7	1	34	2	120	3	123
35 - 39	63	—	2	1	32	1	97	2	99
40 - 44	49	1	1	3	14	1	64	5	69
45 - 49	26	2	1	2	14	1	41	5	46
50 - 54	20	1	5	—	8	—	33	1	34
55 - 59	9	—	5	—	2	—	16	—	16
60 and over	—	—	2	—	—	—	2	—	2
Not known	2	—	1	—	3	—	6	—	6
Totals	422	4	60	25	147	11	629	40	669

**Table 8.1B — All employees at July 1973.
Age and sex distribution: percentages**

Age group	Hourly Rated	Clerical	Salaried	Total		
	Total	Total	Total	male	female	total
15 - 19	0.9	22.6	0.6	2.9	15.0	3.6
20 - 24	17.7	26.2	8.4	15.9	27.5	16.6
25 - 29	22.4	15.5	20.6	21.3	17.5	21.1
30 - 34	18.6	9.5	23.2	19.3	7.5	18.6
35 - 39	14.9	3.6	21.3	15.6	5.0	14.9
40 - 44	11.8	4.8	9.7	10.3	12.5	10.4
45 - 49	6.6	3.6	9.7	6.6	12.5	6.9
50 - 54	5.0	6.0	5.2	5.3	2.5	5.1
55 - 59	2.1	6.0	1.3	2.6	—	2.4
60 and over	—	2.4	—	0.3	—	0.3
Totals	100.0	100.0·	100.0	100.0	100.0	100.0

concentrated in the 15-64 age groups, i.e. they are all of working age. In this, they are significantly different from the local population, whose age structure was discussed earlier. It would be more apposite, however, to draw the distinctions between the East Ross population and the total population dependent on British Aluminium, i.e. including the families of British Aluminium employees.[1] The relevant age statistics for the latter are set out in Table 8.2.

Table 8.2 — Age distribution of B.A. families

age group	employees	wives[2]	children	totals	percentage distribution
0 - 14	—	—	510	510	25.1
15 - 24	134	92	294	520	25.6
25 - 34	263	236	—	499	24.5
35 - 44	168	152	—	320	15.7
45 - 54	80	74	—	154	7.6
55 - 64	18	14	—	32	1.6
65 +	—	—	—	—	—
Not known	6	4	—	10	—
Totals	669	572	804	2045	100.0

The comparison between this age distribution and that of the local population (as enumerated by the 1971 Census) is given in Table 8.3. The points made earlier regarding the peculiar age structure of the East Ross area — a structure similar with those of most rural areas — are supported by the differences evident from the table. In particular, the East Ross population is shown to be significantly older and significantly under-represented in the 15 - 44 age groups. The establishment of the smelter is obviously one step in the improvement of this age structure. Another interesting point is the large number of children in the B.A. population (giving a percentage share little different from that of the local population) who represent a potentially substantial increase in the labour supply in the near future.

For certain purposes it is probably more interesting to consider the differences between the 'local' B.A. population and the 'inmigrant' B.A. population and these differences are set out in Tables 8.4A and 8.4B. In respect of any conclusions to be drawn regarding the differences between the B. A. population and the local East Ross population, the inmigrant and local B.A. components are very similar. There are some interesting differences, however, between the two groups. Firstly, local B.A.

---

[1] Defined to include children living with the family. The total number of children of B.A. employees was 1081, of whom 804 have been included for present purposes, (see below). Elderly dependents were excluded as their number was believed to be insignificant.

[2] Or husbands, where appropriate.

Table 8.3 — Age distributions: percentage figures

age group	East Ross population	B.A. population
0 - 14	26.1	25.1
15 - 24	13.2	25.6
25 - 34	11.8	24.5
35 - 44	11.8	15.7
45 - 54	11.8	7.6
55 - 64	11.4	1.6
65 +	14.0	0.0
	100.0	100.0

Table 8.4A — Age distribution of local B.A. population

age group	employees	wives	children	total	percentage distribution
0 - 14	—	—	231	231	26.7
15 - 24	61	40	121	222	25.7
25 - 34	117	98	—	215	24.9
35 - 44	63	61	—	124	14.4
45 - 54	27	28	—	55	6.4
55 - 64	12	5	—	17	2.0
65 +	—	—	—	—	0.0
Not known	—	1	—	1	—
	280	233	352	865	100.0

Table 8.4B — Age distribution of inmigrant B.A. population

age group	employees	wives	children	total	percentage distribution
0 - 14	—	—	279	279	23.8
15 - 24	73	52	173	298	25.4
25 - 34	146	138	—	284	24.3
35 - 44	105	91	—	196	16.7
45 - 54	53	46	—	99	8.5
55 - 64	6	9	—	15	1.3
65 +	—	—	—	—	0.0
Not known	6	3	—	9	—
	389	339	452	1180	100.0

employees are slightly younger on average. Secondly, a lower proportion are married (83.0% of 87%). Thirdly, the local B.A. employees have proportionately more children, despite the lower proportion married: local B.A. employees represent 41.9% of the total B.A. employees, but they have 43.8% of the total number of B.A. children. In other words the number of children per each married local employee is higher than the B.A. average. Presumably these differences can be accounted for by the higher proportion of salaried staff among the inmigrant B.A. employees.

The geographical origins of employees are given in Tables 8.5A and 8.5B and 8.6A and 8.6B. Two definitions of geographical origin have been used — residence on application and place of birth. Neither is completely satisfactory but together they probably provide the best definition possible. Residence on application statistics are deceptive to some extent because of the number of people who came to the Invergordon area either to work on the construction of the smelter, and subsequently remained in the hope of obtaining further employment with B.A., or Grampian Chemicals or another company. Place of birth statistics are similarly distorted by return migration but an estimate of the number of return migrants is given below.

Great interest is often engendered in the number of locals employed in such developments as the Invergordon smelter. On the one hand the development agencies concerned — in this case the County Council and the H.I.D.B. — have usually sought to attract firms to the area in order to reduce local unemployment and they are therefore keen that as many local people as possible should be employed. Forebodings are often made about the large proportion of outsiders who will be brought in, usually for the best and best-paid jobs, and Invergordon was no exception. On the other hand, there are incentives for the company involved to employ as much local labour as possible since by doing so costs of removal will be lessened and turnover rates would probably be lower. In any event the crucial factors are the range of labour skills required, the range of skills possessed by locals and the recruitment procedure of the company. In the case of B.A. it would be fair to say that the company endeavoured to recruit locally as far as was possible and this is reflected, for example, in the geographical distribution of recruitment advertising mentioned above. To what extent they were successful can be seen from the following tables. Presumably whether or not the distributions are regarded as satisfactory depends on subjective judgement and B.A. have attracted both praise and criticism for the number of locals they have employed. Certainly, in comparison with similar developments elsewhere, the proportion of locals is high.

The "local area" for the purposes of the present study is East Ross, which comprises "Invergordon burgh and district" and "East Ross (remainder)" in the tables. In terms of residence on application, 280 or 43% of all employees at July 1973 could be regarded therefore as locals. Significant differences are apparent among the three groups: 47.7% of hourly rated, 75.3% of clerical and only 12.5% of salaried employees are locals. As regards hourly rated and clerical employees virtually everybody came from Scotland but 30.3% of the salaried staff were living elsewhere in the U.K. when they applied. The place of birth statistics present a different pattern: 170 (24.6%) of the 669 employees were born in East Ross; and these comprised 26.0% of hourly rated 55.4% of clerical and 4.5% of salaried employees. It is interesting to note, however, that another 152 employees were born in other parts of the Highlands and Islands and altogether 88% were born in Scotland. Again the differences among the various groups are as might be expected: 91.0% of hourly rated employees were born in Scotland; 95.2% of clerical; and 75.0% of salaried employees.

If changes in these patterns over time are considered, it is obvious that there were external influences which affect the geographical pattern of recruitment. Regarding residence on application, 59.9% of all first phase employees (as at August '71) were local, compared with only 31.3% of second phase employees. 58.0% of first phase continuees were locals. The respective figures for place of birth were: 33.9% of all first phase and 16.8% of second phase employees; and 34.5% of first phase continuees were born locally.

Table 8.5A — All employees at July 1973. Residence on application

Area	Hourly Rated	Clerical	Salaried	Total
Invergordon burgh and district	84	22	6	112
East Ross (remainder)	113	42	13	168
Moray Firth	25	7	11	43
Highlands	58	6	19	83
Scotland	106	4	56	166
United Kingdom	20	3	46	69
Rest of the world	7	1	1	9
Not known	13	—	6	19
Totals	426	85	158	669

Table 8.5B — All employees at July 1973. Residence on application Percentage distribution

Area	Hourly Rated	Clerical	Salaried	Total
Invergordon burgh and district	20.3	25.9	3.9	17.2
East Ross (remainder)	27.4	49.4	8.6	25.8
Moray Firth	6.1	8.2	7.2	6.6
Highlands	14.0	7.1	12.5	12.8
Scotland	25.7	4.7	36.8	25.5
United Kingdom	4.8	3.5	30.3	10.6
Rest of the world	1.7	1.2	0.7	1.4
Totals	100.0	100.0	100.0	100.0

The obvious explanation for this changing pattern is that B.A. found it difficult to recruit locally as Highlands Fabricators and MK-Shand began to recruit. A cursory examination of the fall of numbers unemployed over the period supports such an explanation. The available information suggests that these recruitment difficulties applied particularly to the hourly rate production employees.

An interesting phenomenon that has arisen in connection with the B.A. smelter has been the evidence of return migration, i.e. people who had originally left the area and have now returned. Taking the definition of locals by residence at time of application (see above) it was stated that 280 could be regarded as locals and 389 as inmigrants: of the latter it is estimated that 88 were return migrants, i.e. 22.6% of all the incomers.

Table 8.6A All employees at July 1973. Place of birth

Area	Hourly Rated	Clerical	Salaried	Total
Invergordon burgh and district	21	8	2	31
East Ross (remainder)	86	38	5	129
Moray Firth	19	17	8	44
Highlands	81	8	19	108
Scotland	169	8	83	260
United Kingdom	22	4	38	64
Rest of the world	13	—	1	14
Not known	15	2	2	19
Totals	426	85	158	669

**Table 8.6B — All employees at July 1973. Place of birth
Percentage distribution**

Area	Hourly Rated	Clerical	Salaried	Total
Invergordon burgh and district	5.1	9.6	1.3	4.8
East Ross (remainder)	20.9	45.8	3.2	19.8
Moray Firth	4.6	20.5	5.1	6.8
Highlands	19.7	9.6	12.2	16.6
Scotland	41.1	9.6	53.2	40.0
United Kingdom	5.4	4.8	24.4	9.8
Rest of the world	3.6	—	0.6	2.2
Totals	100.0	100.0	100.0	100.0

Alternatively if residence two years prior to application was used, 197 were residing locally and 472 were inmigrants; and of the latter 113 were return migrants i.e. 23.9% of all incomers. The inclusion of return migrants with local residents would increase the proportion of locals to 54.7% (using the definition of residence at time of application) or 46.3% (using the definition of residence two years prior).

This group of employees at B.A. represent not only a sizeable number but also merit attention greater than their numbers. It was mentioned in the first section of this report that one of the main problems of the Highlands and Islands was the steady emigration of people to other areas of the U.K. and to other countries. The underlying premise of policy therefore has been to reduce this emigration by providing adequate employment opportunities for the local population and by attracting back to the area people who had emigrated. This presupposes that the main cause (or a major cause) was the lack of suitable employment opportunities — and that once these were provided people would return.

Economic theories suggest two main theories of the causes of the decision to migrate, firstly the push factor of dissatisfaction with local conditions (either economic or non-economic, or indeed both) and the pull factor of the area of destination, e.g. lower unemployment and higher earnings. It is generally believed that only when the net strength of the push factor is positive (i.e. taking account of the actual costs of migration) will the potential migrant become an actual migrant. Similarly, return migration will only occur when the balance of costs and benefits, actual or perceived, is changing in favour of the area of origin.

Return migration is important because return migrants usually have a great deal more information about conditions in their area of origin than non-return migrants. "Psychic determinants in many cases overshadowed purely pecuniary considerations, where psychic variables included proxies for strength of ties in country of origin and the difficulty of adjustment in country of destination. Reversing the direction of movement, however, alters the relative importance since the destination is now terra cognito."[3] Evidence on the relative importance of the various factors is very difficult to obtain and quantify.

As part of the present study a survey was undertaken of school leavers from the local schools and some of the results may be of relevance. One question asked of those school leavers who had left the Invergordon area concerned their reasons for leaving and 79% of respondants (excluding students) stated that the main reason was the lack of suitable employment opportunities. Approximately 10% mentioned family reasons and a similar proportion a dislike of the area. Including students some 66% said that they would return to work in the area if suitable opportunities were available. It should also be mentioned that over 70% of all respondants regarded local employment opportunities as "poor" or "very poor".

The response may not be typical of the whole population of East Ross and emigrants from the area but such views do appear to be widely held. Of the 88 return migrants identified above, 64 said that they had left the

---

[3] Y. Comay: *Determinants of return migration: Canadian professionals in the United States* in *Southern Economic Journal* (1971)

area because of poor local opportunities relative to opportunities else-where. The return migrants were asked to rank their reasons for return and 53 had returned because of the improvement in local employment opport-unities, 23 were dissatisfied elsewhere and 10 gave other reasons. This gives the impression that the "pull" factor of East Ross is greater than the "push" factor of other areas but it should be remembered that the number of migrants returning to the area to work with B.A. is a very small proportion of the total number of emigrants who have left the area and are presently residing elsewhere. If the East Ross economy experiences a long-run improvement, then it is certain that return migration will increase. In similar cases it has been very important. Vanderkemp, for example, has shown that in Canada during the period 1956-61 about half of all migration consisted of return movement.[4] Miller's study of migration in the United States during the period 1955-60 produced a much lower proportion — 14.6% of total migration across State boundaries — but for some States it was much higher: e.g. 44.0% of migrants in West Virginia were return migrants, 38.2% in Arkansas, 36.8% in Mississippi and 35.2% in Kentucky.[5] Miller concludes, however, that "the effect of return migration is to make the short-term response of inmigration to improved economic conditions greater than the long term . . . if economic conditions remain good, the effect is also to reduce outmigration. Both this and the increased return migration reduce the pull of ex-residents who might move back. The result is that after the passage of many years the inmigration rate must decline." Nevertheless, it would be reasonable to expect that over the next few years return migration could provide the substantial proportion of an increased labour supply, not only in the East Ross area but in other areas of the Highlands and Islands.

Another interesting factor concerns those B.A. employees who have moved from other areas of the Highlands. It was suggested in the first section of this report that if Invergordon was built up as a major growth centre, it might stem the flow of population from the region by attracting people from other areas who would otherwise have left the region altogether. Tables 8.5 and 8.6 show that 12.8% of the smelter's employees were residing elsewhere in the region at the time of application and 16.6% had been born elsewhere in the region. These are sizeable proportions in the present context but it is too early to know whether or not Invergordon is attracting people who would otherwise have left the Highlands and Islands. On the other hand, most of the employees from the rest of the region come from Sutherland and Caithness and this labour loss, combined with similar losses to the oil-related developments in East Ross, may well cause serious problems in such areas.

Tables 8.7A and 8.7B and 8.8A and 8.8B give the previous industry and occupation of the 669 permanent employees. In terms of industrial origins, B.A. recruited from a wide range of industries, the most important being construction (17.0%), metal manufacture (12.7%), transport and com-munication (5.8%), distributive trades (5.7%), agriculture, forestry and fishing (5.2%) and food, drink and tobacco (4.9%). In addition 74 people

[4] J. Vanderkemp: *Interregional mobility in Canada: a study of the time pattern of migration* in *Canadian Journal of Economics* (1968)
[5] E. Miller: *Return and non-return inmigration* in *Growth and Change* (1973)

Table 8.7A — All employees at July 1973. Employment (by industry) prior to joining B.A.

Order No.	Industry	Standard Industrial Classification, 1968			
		Hourly Rated	Clerical	Salaried	Total
I	Agriculture, forestry, fishing	29	2	4	35
II	Mining and quarrying	8	—	5	13
III	Food, drink and tobacco	25	3	4	32
IV	Coal and petroleum products	3	1	2	6
V	Chemicals and allied	8	1	4	13
VI	Metal manufacture	17	5	63	85
VII	Mechanical engineering	17	—	9	26
VIII	Instrument engineering	10	—	4	14
IX	Electrical engineering	8	—	2	10
X	Shipbuilding	9	—	3	12
XI	Vehicles	1	—	4	5
XII	Metal goods not elsewhere specified	—	—	—	—
XIII	Textiles	1	—	1	2
XIV	Leather etc.	—	—	—	—
XV	Clothing and footwear	—	—	—	—
XVI	Bricks, pottery etc.	3	—	1	4
XVII	Timber, furniture etc.	6	1	1	8
XVIII	Paper, printing and publishing	2	1	3	6
XIX	Other manufacturing	—	—	—	—
XX	Construction	91	17	6	114
XXI	Gas, electricity and water	8	2	4	14
XXII	Transport and communication	29	4	6	39
XXIII	Distributive trades	28	7	3	38
XXIV	Insurance, banking etc.	3	2	3	8
XXV	Professional and scientific	4	9	13	26
XXVI	Miscellaneous services	20	1	1	22
XXVII	Public administration and defence	16	11	5	32
	Not known	4	1	1	6
	Unemployed	74	2	3	79
	No previous employment	2	15	3	20
	Totals	426	85	158	669

had been unemployed prior to taking up employment with B.A. This particular distribution obviously reflects the distribution of economic activity in the local area and the effects of labour losses on local industries are discussed below. It will be seen from the tables that there are significant differences among the various categories of employees but these are largely self-explanatory.

In view of the company's desire to recruit people with relatively stable employment records, data was obtained on the number of jobs held in the previous five years. The information collected showed that 70.6% of employees had had only one or two jobs during that period. The proportions for clerical and salaried staff were even higher — 75.2% and 88.0% — and it is interesting to note that 11.5% of all employees had been with their previous firms for more than 10 years.

There are some signs that these patterns have changed since the first recruitment stages, and this is exemplified by the turnover data. The monthly turnover percentages in Table 8.9 below are the numbers leaving each month as a percentage of the numbers employed at the end of each month, and a distinction was made between salaried and hourly rated staff. Over the period January 1971 and May 1973 a steadily increasing trend in turnover can be seen with the average monthly percentages in 1971 being 1.02%, in 1972 2.32% and in the first part of 1973 2.60%. Apart from the usual seasonal fluctuations the increase in turnover experienced by B.A. coincides closely with the build-up of employment at Highlands Fabricators and MK-Shand and in such circumstances of substantially increased competition in the local labour market, increased turnover rates were to be expected. Certainly, turnover was very low during the first year of operation (particularly as the normal experience for new plants is high turnover to begin with and then a steady fall as production and the labour force settle down), which probably bears testament to the detailed planning during and before the construction phase. During 1971 and 1972 turnover was higher among locals than non-locals and there was a discernible trend of people returning to their former occupations particularly in agriculture. Subsequently, however, the main problem became the shortage of accommodation, which made it difficult to recruit and retain people from outwith the area. In the face of labour losses and recruitment difficulties, B.A. were forced to provide a caravan site adjacent to the smelter as a temporary measure and, not unexpectedly, there was a high turnover of employees and families living on the site. Sufficient permanent housing has now become available for the caravan site to be closed and there has been a steady return of labour from Highlands Fabricators and MK-Shand, probably as a consequence of the nature of the work and the uncertainties surrounding those companies' long-term futures in East Ross. From the point of view of B.A. the position now appears to have settled down after a period of difficulty largely arising from the increased competition for labour and the acute shortage of housing.

Turning to the wider impact on the local labour market, the most sensitive measure is the level of unemployment. In the chapter on the construction phase it was shown (Table 6.4) that unemployment fell sharply during construction but then rose again as activity ran down. Table 8.10 gives the percentage unemployment figures for the period 1971-1974 together with the ratios of the Invergordon:Scotland figures and the

Table 8.7B — All employees at July 1973. Employment (by industry) prior to joining B.A. Percentage Distribution

Order No.	Industry	Standard Industrial Classification, 1968			
		Hourly Rated	Clerical	Salaried	Total
I	Agriculture, forestry, fishing	8.4	3.0	2.6	6.2
II	Mining and quarrying	2.3	—	3.3	2.3
III	Food, drink and tobacco	7.2	4.5	2.5	5.7
IV	Coal and petroleum products	0.9	1.5	1.3	1.1
V	Chemicals and allied	2.3	1.5	2.6	2.3
VI	Metal manufacture	4.9	7.5	41.7	15.1
VII	Mechanical engineering	4.9	—	6.0	4.6
VIII	Instrument engineering	2.9	—	2.6	2.5
IX	Electrical engineering	2.3	—	1.3	1.8
X	Shipbuilding	2.6	—	2.0	2.1
XI	Vehicles	0.3	—	2.6	0.9
XII	Metal goods not elsewhere specified	—	—	—	—
XIII	Textiles	0.3	—	0.7	0.4
XIV	Leather etc.	—	—	—	—
XV	Clothing and footwear	—	—	—	—
XVI	Bricks, pottery etc.	0.9	—	0.7	0.7
XVII	Timber, furniture etc.	1.7	1.5	0.7	1.4
XVIII	Paper, printing and publishing	0.6	1.5	2.0	1.1
XIX	Other manufacturing	—	—	—	—
XX	Construction	26.3	25.4	4.0	20.2
XXI	Gas, electricity and water	2.3	3.0	2.6	2.5
XXII	Transport and communication	8.4	6.0	4.0	6.9
XXIII	Distributive trades	8.1	10.4	2.0	6.7
XXIV	Insurance, banking etc.	0.9	3.0	2.0	1.4
XXV	Professional and scientific	1.2	13.4	8.6	4.6
XXVI	Miscellaneous services	5.8	1.5	0.7	3.9
XXVII	Public administration and defence	4.6	16.4	3.3	5.7
	Totals	100.0	100.0	100.0	100.0

Table 8.8A — All employees at July 1973. Occupation prior to joining B.A.

Order No.	Occupation	Classification of Occupations, 1972			
		Hourly Rated	Clerical	Salaried	Total
I	Managerial: general	—	—	4	4
II	Professional: managerial and administration	—	—	73	73
III	Professional: education, health etc.	1	2	3	6
IV	Literary, artistic and sports	2	—	1	3
V	Professional: science, engineering etc.	5	—	9	14
VI	Managerial: other than general	3	—	8	11
VII	Clerical	11	34	4	49
VIII	Selling	19	6	11	36
IX	Security	10	6	1	17
X	Catering, personal service etc.	17	13	3	33
XI	Farming and fishing	34	2	3	39
XII	Materials processing (excluding metal)	24	1	4	29
XIII	Making and repairing (excluding metal and electrical)	25	—	2	27
XIV	Processing etc. (metal and electrical)	128	1	22	151
XV	Painting etc.	4	1	—	5
XVI	Construction and mining	93	2	—	95
XVII	Transport operating etc.	39	2	3	44
XVIII	Miscellaneous	2	—	3	5
	No previous occupation	—	15	1	16
	Not known	9	—	3	12
	Totals	426	85	158	669

Table 8.8B — All employees at July 1973. Occupation prior to joining B.A. Percentage distribution

Order No.	Occupation	Classification of Occupations, 1972			
		Hourly Rated	Clerical	Salaried	Total
I	Managerial: general	—	—	2.6	0.6
II	Professional: managerial and administration	—	—	47.1	11.1
III	Professional: education, health, etc.	0.2	2.4	1.9	0.9
IV	Literary, artistic and sports	0.5	—	0.6	0.5
V	Professional: science, engineering etc.	1.2	—	5.8	2.1
VI	Managerial: other than general	0.7	—	5.2	1.7
VII	Clerical	2.7	40.0	2.6	7.5
VIII	Selling	4.6	7.1	7.1	5.5
IX	Security	2.4	7.1	0.6	2.6
X	Catering, personal service etc.	4.1	15.3	1.9	5.2
XI	Farming and fishing	8.2	2.4	1.9	5.9
XII	Materials processing (excluding metal)	5.8	1.2	2.6	4.4
XIII	Making and repairing (excluding metal and electrical)	6.0	—	1.3	4.1
XIV	Processing etc. (metal and electrical)	30.8	1.2	14.2	23.0
XV	Painting etc.	1.0	1.2	—	0.8
XVI	Construction and mining	22.4	2.4	—	14.5
XVII	Transport operating etc.	9.4	2.4	1.9	6.7
XVIII	Miscellaneous	0.5	—	1.9	0.8
	No previous occupation	—	17.6	0.6	2.4
	Totals	100.0	100.0	100.0	100.0

marked improvement since March 1972 is obvious; but since B.A.'s second phase recruitment was largely completed by January 1973 there can be no doubt that the improvement was attributable to employment growth at Highlands Fabricators and MK-Shand — and that subsequent deteriorations in the situation are attributable to the fluctuations in those companies' labour forces. It was noted earlier that 79 of B.A.'s 669 employees in July 1973 had been unemployed immediately prior to working at the smelter and some of the jobs vacated by people leaving to work at the smelter would have been filled by the unemployed — an estimated 80 to 100 on available information.

Table 8.9 — Percentage turnover rates, 1971-73

	1971	1972	1973
January	0.00	3.27	2.10
February	1.45	0.69	3.10
March	1.07	1.16	2.70
April	0.91	2.76	2.70
May	0.84	5.00	2.40
June	1.55	2.00	
July	0.77	0.87	
August	1.46	1.87	
September	1.68	2.62	
October	1.17	2.90	
November	0.68	1.95	
December	0.68	2.70	

Table 8.10 — Unemployment data, 1971-74

	1971	1972	1973	1974
A. TOTAL				
January	8.6	12.9	5.7	4.0
February	8.4	12.6	5.5	3.5
March	8.4	11.3	4.9	3.2
April	8.3	9.4	4.8	3.2
May	7.7	7.4	4.7	2.7
June	8.4	5.5	5.0	3.0
July	9.8	4.7	5.0	3.2
August	10.9	4.8	5.1	2.7
September	11.3	5.0	4.2	3.3
October	11.8	4.6	4.2	3.7
November	13.1	5.2	3.6	*
December	12.3	6.1	3.7	*
B. RATIOS TO SCOTTISH FIGURES				
January	1.62	1.82	0.93	0.89
February	1.55	1.25	0.98	0.80
March	1.47	1.57	0.92	0.76
April	1.46	1.32	0.89	0.69
May	1.38	1.16	1.02	0.73
June	1.50	0.90	1.16	0.83
July	1.58	0.72	1.11	0.76
August	1.73	0.73	1.16	0.62
September	1.82	0.74	1.02	0.80
October	1.87	0.74	1.11	0.95
November	2.02	0.88	0.95	*
December	1.89	0.88	1.00	*

* not available
Source: Department of Employment

9 Summary and conclusions

The situation in East Ross has changed so much during the 1970s that it is very difficult to isolate and assess the effects of one particular development. Indeed, the aluminium smelter has not been able to produce yet under normal operating conditions — either because of local labour and housing conditions or the state of the world aluminium industry — and it may well be a few more years before its long-term contribution to the local economy can be evaluated properly.

Nevertheless, the purpose of this study has been to consider in as much detail as possible the effects of both the construction and operating phases of the smelter on the East Ross economy, with particular emphasis on the effects on the local labour market. The use of an input-output model enabled detailed estimates to be made of the effects on the various sectors of the local economy, which is a great advantage over more conventional impact studies in that it shows dearly the differential impact from sector to sector. In impact studies of this type it is essential to separate the results from their interpretation. In the main, the use of an input-output model enables an objective and value-free assessment to be made. The evaluation of such an assessment is an additional and subsequent stage, which is influenced by objectives and local needs, and it is in this respect that opinions may differ on the range of effects.

For example, it is not universally accepted that an expansion of manufacturing activity contributes to the solution of the problems of declining rural areas and when new developments are proposed in such areas there are often vociferous objections, as indeed was the case with the Invergordon smelter. However, the stated objectives of most of the bodies concerned with the economic well-being of East Ross, notably Ross and Cromarty County Council and the Highlands and Islands Development Board, were to try to stem and reverse depopulation and unemployment by attracting new manufacturing activity and it is in this light that the impact assessment of the smelter should be seen. This is not to deny that it is essential at an early stage to consider both the desirability and feasibility of attracting new manufacturing activity to the Highlands and Islands and this was done in the first section of this report. The view was expressed strongly that in the case of East Ross attempts to attract large-scale industry as a· general policy were very desirable and such a view was undoubtedly shared by the great majority of local inhabitants, although some differed on the scale and type of industry which would be desirable and on the particular locations for industrial sites and new housing within the area.

The attraction of large-scale industry was made easier by the substantial physical advantages of the north shore of the Cromarty Firth — in particular, deep water, flat land, reasonably good communications and an adequate labour pool. Whether or not these advantages in their own right would have attracted industry is an impossible question to answer and the opinion has been expressed that, as with the oil-related developments, the smelter would have come to Invergordon without the promotional efforts of the bodies involved; but it is undeniable that these efforts, and the publicity aroused, brought East Ross to the attention of many people who might otherwise have not considered it. It is probably true, also, that the identification of certain appropriate types of industry allowed efforts to be concentrated in a few key sectors, with eventual success. A selective approach is preferable for all similar areas, although in practice many areas may have no choice regarding the type of activity which they can attract, and in the Moray Firth the earlier feasibility studies made some selection possible. If one had to rank the factors which contributed to the establishment of British Aluminium at Invergordon, however, the feasibility studies and promotional efforts would have a significantly lower value than the state of the world aluminium industry and B.A.'s U.K. operations, but without them it is likely that a site other than Invergordon would have been chosen.

The main aspects considered in this study have been the changes in output and employment, but probably the best indicator of the improvement in the area's economic health is the extent of population change. In Chapter 2 it was shown that one of the most serious problems was depopulation and that the population in 1968 was less than it had been in 1951. As can be seen from Table 9.1 the trends have been reversed sharply and there was a 5,000 increase (17.1%) in population during the period 1968-74. The table uses the Registrar-General's annual estimates rather than the decennial census data because the former provide figures for each year on a consistent basis.

The 1974 estimates almost certainly understate the position because of the many difficulties in estimating the numbers living in temporary accommodation and the ususal difficulties in estimating the populations of small areas should be borne in mind. Nevertheless, the main trends are clear. From 1968-71 the population of East Ross increased by approximately 1,600, mainly due to the smelter, and from 1971-74 by another 3,400, mainly due to Highlands Fabricators and MK-Shand. Within the area the population of all the burghs except Cromarty grew substantially, with the largest increases in Invergordon and Tain, as would be expected. The population of Cromarty appears to have fallen until 1972 and it is clear that Cromarty and the Black Isle in general were largely unaffected by the smelter because of their relative isolation, and it is only since the inception of a ferry from Nigg to Cromarty that any significant direct effects of the industrial developments on the north shore of the firth have been felt in the Black Isle.

The populations of some of the rural districts also continued to fall but overall this was compensated for by sharp increases in the districts most affected by the developments, in particular Invergordon (+53.0%) and Dingwall (+28.3%), although the Invergordon district increase is inflated by the boundary change with the burgh. Alness village, where most of the local authority housing for smelter employees was built, straddles the boundary line (the River Alness) between the Invergordon and Dingwall districts but most of the housing was on the west (Dingwall) side of the river.

Most of the population increase came through inmigration because natural increase was very low. The death rate in East Ross is significantly higher than in Scotland as a whole and it will take some years before the

Table 9.1 — Population change, 1968-74

	1968	1969	1970	1971	1972	1973	1974	% change 1968-74
Small burghs								
Cromarty	585	587	584	507	488	492	503	-14.0
Dingwall	3,906	3,912	4,171	4,133	4,192	4,275	4,379	+12.1
Fortrose	996	1,027	1,037	1,087	1,088	1,150	1,192	+19.7
Invergordon	1,948	2,074	2,583	2,218*	2,323	2,385	2,454	+26.0
Tain	1,716	1,719	1,770	1,984	2,010	2,057	2,151	+25.3
Total	9,151	9,319	10,145	9,929	10,101	10,359	10,679	+16.7
Districts of county								
Avoch	3,078	3,095	3,058	2,885	2,893	2,907	2,962	-3.8
Dingwall	4,115	3,937	3,935	4,211	4,558	5,007	5,280	+28.3
Fearn	2,181	2,156	2,153	2,138	2,134	2,210	2,597	+19.1
Fortrose	1,040	1,017	955	901	895	902	920	-11.5
Invergordon	2,974	3,123	3,307	3,852*	3,907	4,217	4,549	+53.0
Muir-of-Ord	5,155	5,232	5,187	5,462	5,513	5,598	5,705	+10.7
Tain	1,582	1,560	1,518	1,534	1,528	1,536	1,584	+0.1
Total	20,125	20,120	20,111	20,983	21,428	22,377	23,597	+17.3
TOTAL	29,276	29,439	30,256	30,912	31,529	32,736	34,276	+17.1

* boundary change
Source: Registrar-General's Annual Estimates

Note: it is not possible to show figures for later years because of local government reorganization.

population structure takes on a more normal pattern. For example, natural increase in each of the years 1968-72 was only 73, 90, 80, 122 and 64 respectively and on the basis of the estimates in Table 9.1 net inmigration must have been approximately 85 in 1968-69 (July to June), 732 in 1969-70, 555 in 1970-71 and 524 in 1971-72.

Turning to other economic indicators, time and data constraints made it impossible to undertake detailed work for each year and efforts were concentrated on obtaining data on the local economic structure for the input-output model for 1968 and 1972. It was felt that these years were reasonably representative of the construction and operating phase respectively. Regarding the permanent operation, it was estimated that the establishment of the smelter increased local output by approximately £5,165,000 in 1972, which in relation to the direct output increases of £4,152,000 is equivalent to an output multiplier of 1.24. Similarly, it was estimated that local personal incomes increased by £1,225,000 with a local income multiplier of 1.37. The main local sectors in which output (and personal incomes and employment) increased were retail distribution, miscellaneous services, local government, public utilities, wholesale distribution and transport.

It was pointed out in Chapter 7, however, that most of these increases came from the consumption expenditures of B.A. employees rather than from interindustry purchases. Indeed, the total indirect increase in local output was only £50,000, compared with an induced increase of £650,000. The low values of the input coefficients in Table 7.1 reflect the lack of local interindustry linkages and the high propensity of most industries to import inputs from outwith the area and, obversely, to export most of their output. In this light it is not surprising that the multiplier effects of the smelter are relatively small: the estimated output multiplier for 1972 was 1.24; the income multiplier was 1.37; and the employment multiplier 1.33.

These multiplier estimates are very important in the context of the long-term economic future of East Ross and its development as a 'growth centre'. If the Invergordon smelter is to act as a catalyst for further growth in the area this is likely to come through B.A.'s backward and forward linkages with other firms in the area. To date these have been very weak, however, and given the structure of the U.K. aluminium industry, as summarised in Chapter 3, there are few reasons to expect these linkages to be strengthened — at least in the foreseeable future. At one time, for example, there were high local hopes that a bauxite plant would be built adjacent to the smelter but this is now very unlikely.

In the conclusions to Chapter 4 it was argued that there is a great deal of confusion about the nature and role of growth centres, with the result that an inadequate theoretical construct has been translated into a common policy tool. When Perroux, the founding father of growth centre theory observed that "growth does not appear everywhere at the same time; it appears in growth points or growth poles with varying intensity; it advances by different channels and with varying final effects for the whole economy",[1] he was concerned with economic space rather than geographic space. "As a field of forces economic space consists of centres (or poles, or foci) from which centrifugal forces emanate and to which centrifugal forces are attracted".[2] The important features of a growth centre are the existence of important interindustry linkages among firms who are members of fast-growing industries, and size and geographical location are relatively unimportant. The impetus to additional growth comes from the creation of both external and internal economies and, again, this is

[1] F. Perroux: *Note sur la notion de pole de croissance* in *Economic Applique* (1955)
[2] F. Perroux: *Economic space: theory and application* in *Quarterly Journal of Economics* (1950)

largely related to the particular complex of firms involved. There may well be some external economies created by the establishment of a few large but unconnected activities but these would be much less than those arising from a complex of interlinked industries.

The clear implication for Invergordon is that if it is to act as a major growth centre in the Highlands and Islands it needs over time to attract related industries and to build up the linkages with local firms. There are signs of this happening in Aberdeen within the complex of oil and gas-related activities but the type and likely permanence of the oil-related developments in East Ross are very different and the multiplier effects are probably of the same magnitude as those of the aluminium smelter.

It would probably be a reasonable assessment to say that generally those involved with the promotion of growth centre policies have become disillusioned with their apparent lack of success. Certainly, such policies are not as popular as they were in the 1960s. Richardson gives a number of reasons for this: "The most dominant and universal factor has been the failure of the growth poles to stimulate area-wide regional development. Many have functioned as 'enclaves' with closer links with the national and international economies outside the region. Spatial spillovers within the region have been either minimal or strongly negative".[3]

Richardson goes on to argue, however, as Parr has also done recently[4], that much of this criticism is premature in that it now appears to take much longer, probably 15-25 years, for the beneficial effects of growth centres to be firmly established in a region. Parr suggested a sequence of three phases in the generation of spread and back wash effects: firstly, a period of favourable effects, due to increased hinterland production, commuting, favourable labour migration flows and increased service provision; secondly, an unfavourable phase with more centralized production and selective migration causing problems in the hinterland; and a final beneficial phase with renewed decentralization of economic activity and increased demand for the products of the hinterland.

Unfortunately there is little empirical evidence at the present time to support the arguments of these two authors but they do appear to have some relevance to the Invergordon situation. It could well be that Invergordon is currently in the middle phase, with unfavourable effects being dominant, and that over time the balance of benefits and costs will change, particularly as local firms increase their productive capacities to take advantage of new opportunities. It will be a few years, however, before any assessment of this can be made.

In that light, it is necessary to mention briefly the effects on the more out-lying parts of the geographical area affected, notably Sutherland and Caithness to the north. In those districts the general economic state is much worse than in East Ross and most attempts to introduce manufacturing industry to alleviate serious economic problems have been unsuccessful. There are strong local worries that the developments in East Ross will exacerbate the problems. Both Highlands Fabricators and MK-Shand

---

[3] H.W. Richardson: *Growth pole spillovers: the dynamics of backwash and spread, Regional Studies*, vol. 10., no.1 (1976), pp. 1-9
[4] J.B. Parr: *Growth poles, regional development and central place theory, Papers of the Regional Science Association*, vol. 31 (1973), pp. 173-212.

employ fairly large numbers of people from these districts, most of whom commute daily, but they have been recruited largely from the few remaining manufacturing firms and there is a danger that some may close down.

Turning to employment, it was estimated in Chapter 7 that in 1972 in addition to the smelter's 550 employees another 180 or so indirect and induced jobs had been created in other sectors of the local economy, almost entirely in the service industries. This represents the gross increase in employment and has to be offset by any job destruction in local industries. The current number employed at the smelter is just over 800.

Detailed studies were done of the geographical, industrial and occupational origins of the smelter's permanent labour force in August 1971 when the number of employees was 404 and in July 1973 when the number had increased to 669. The results for the latter group were summarized in Chapter 8. As regards geographical origins, two definitions were used: by residence at the time of application for employment, 43% of all employees were living in East Ross and could therefore be regarded as locals; by place of birth, 24.6% of employees were local. These proportions were lower than those for the August 1971 labour force but the simple explanation is that B.A. found it more difficult to recruit locally as the oil developments began to expand. There was also evidence of significant return migration to the area by people who had previously left to work elsewhere.

Given the sophisticated technology of the smelter and the virtual absence of manufacturing activity in East Ross, the number of locals recruited is encouragingly high and there has been relatively little turnover among local employees. In part this is due to the success of B.A.'s training programmes and in part to the surprising adaptability of the local labour force, particularly those with previous experience in agriculture and fishing. Both Highlands Fabricators and MK-Shand have been similarly surprised by the quality of labour in the area and as a whole training programmes have proved worthwhile. It would be impossible to generalise for the whole of the Highlands and Islands, or indeed for other rural areas, but certainly in the case of East Ross the lack of labour experience of large-scale manufacturing activity has not been a drawback and the adaptability of people previously engaged in farming and fishing occupations, for example, exceeded expectations.

The other main conclusion of the labour force studies concerns the industrial origins, largely in relation to the recruitment from local firms. The danger of substantial job destruction in indigenous industries is always a real one in such cases and fears were expressed prior to the advent of B.A. about the long-term threats to local industry through labour losses. Unfortunately, it is a frequent assumption that the main labour source for a new development will be the unemployed but this is very unrealistic. In the case of the Invergordon smelter, of the 669 employees in the 1973 survey only 74 people had been unemployed immediately prior to taking up employment, 41 of them locals. In 1968 the average number of registered unemployed was 569, 1969 - 486, 1970 - 420m 1971 - 779 and 1972 - 595, so it can be seen that the smelter had little direct impact on the unemployment register, except during the construction phase. About 80 of the jobs vacated by smelter employees, however, were immediately filled by unemployed people and there is always a chain reaction which takes a long time to complete.

The local industries most affected by labour losses were agriculture, whisky distilling, construction, transport and miscellaneous services, although it should be stressed that some industries had already lost labour to the smelter's construction force. Detailed discussions were held with most of the local firms affected and the general feeling was that the problems had not been serious and solutions had been found. One of the main reasons was that some sectors were able and willing to reduce employment in that the processes of economic change had left them with more employees than they needed and it is an interesting fact that in some parts of the retail sector employment fell sharply with little effect on output and efficiency. The agricultural labour force, for example, declined by an average 6.5% per year over the period 1968-72 but this was not significantly different from the rest of the U.K. and there are signs that the pressure of industrial development induced some welcome reforms in agricultural practice, which had been slow in coming to East Ross. Greater use has also been made of specialist contractors and relief services and a recent study concluded that "under conditions where labour is scarce farming systems will be evolved which require less labour".[5] Indeed, the labour losses to the smelter's permanent labour force were small, under 25, although of the construction labour force between 80 and 110 had been employed in the local agricultural sector.

In most cases, other industries adapted similarly, with the worst-hit being public transport and construction, and the main effect of the increased competition for labour was to drive up local wage rates, which in view of their relatively low levels during the 1960s was generally regarded as welcome. It should be pointed out, however, that the problems caused by the oil-related developments have been much greater and, coupled with the national economic recession, some local firms have not been able to find adequate and long-term solutions.

One final point regarding the recruitment of the permanent labour force is that the distribution of employees by age (Table 8.1) is of interest in the context of the employment of young people. As was pointed out in Chapter 2, there was widespread agreement that one of the serious local problems was the continuing emigration of young people and one of the common hopes for the smelter was that it would stem the outflow of brighter school-leavers. Clearly, this has not been the case since only 24 (3.6%) of permanent employees were under 20 years of age. On reflection, this is not surprising because of the smelter's labour requirements and recruitment practices, although two small apprenticeship schemes are operated. The main improvement in job opportunities for local school leavers came by way of those vacated by people leaving to join B.A. A few of the larger employers thought seriously about improving and expanding apprenticeship schemes to ensure a supply of skilled labour in the future, but these plans were largely frustrated by the advent of Highlands Fabricators and MK-Shand. On the whole, the changes have brought more of the tradit-

---

[5] See J. Ormiston: *Moray Firth: an agricultural study* (1973)

ional jobs available but very few new ones, with the exception of school teachers and other local authority posts. It seems reasonable to conclude, therefore, that the smelter has had only a limited impact on the opportunities for school-leavers, particularly the brighter ones, and indeed the inmigration of young people with children will eventually mean an increase in the number of school-leavers, so there is still a great need in East Ross for an improvement in certain types of employment opportunities. Similarly, given that B.A. and the oil-related firms employ largely male labour, there is a great need for more jobs for females, although they have been moving into some occupations traditionally reserved for males.

From the local authority side the task of accommodating the smelter was made easier by a special set of organizational arrangements dealing with physical planning, housebuilding etc. and by the fact that the public inquiry system gave them plenty advance warning. The intention of the special arrangements was to coordinate the activities of the various local and central government bodies involved and of B.A. and its various contractors, and the main vehicle used was the Invergordon Steering Group. Both to those involved and to interested observers, this appears to have been a very useful body and the arrangements may well be worth repeating in similar situations. One of the main tasks of the Invergordon Steering Group was to coordinate the provision of housing and other infrastructure and this was done surprisingly smoothly, in the light of the difficulties of obtaining labour during the smelter's construction phase. Most of the local authority houses for smelter employees were built at Alness, a few miles west of Invergordon, and a great deal of detailed work went into the design and planning. In the case of the smelter it was relatively easy to forecast the numbers of houses, school places and so forth required and it was only with the advent of the oil-related developments that the housing position became very difficult.

Within Ross and Cromarty County Council itself, a special East Ross Working Group was formed — as part of the planning and development departments — to deal with the problems generated by rapid industrial growth but eventually this group ran into difficulties not only with its forecasts but with internal politics within the council. Generally, however, it would be a fair conclusion that with regard to the smelter itself, the infrastructure provision went smoothly and, apart from the issues of principle raised at the public inquiries regarding the loss of agricultural land, the only serious complaints concerned the lack of provision of social amenities.[6]

In conclusion, therefore, the aluminium smelter has brought a substantial improvement in the economic fortunes of East Ross, through the provision of over 700 secure and well-paid jobs in an area which was previously experiencing depopulation and high unemployment. The problems of establishing a large industrial plant in a rural area were alleviated by the special planning arrangements made and by British Aluminium's determination to integrate its activities and those of its employees with the local community and economy. Both appear to be a

---

[6] See A. Currie and associates: *The objectives of Highland development: an Easter Ross case study* (1973)

good model for comparable situations. Some local industries benefitted from the increase in output and incomes, mainly those in the service sector, whilst others suffered from the loss of good agricultural land and labour, although in most cases the latter difficulties were resolved adequately. The most serious problems came during the construction phase and it is important to note that, because the construction labour force was considerably greater than the permanent labour force, the level of unemployment in the area was higher after the smelter began operations than before. This problem was alleviated by the advent of oil-related developments but it is likely to recur and it is essential to remember that one large industrial plant does not constitute a growth centre and can only solve a limited number of problems. In particular, from a long-term point of view there is still a great need in the area for more employment for females and school-leavers. The Invergordon smelter has given the local economy a broader and firmer base on which to build industrial growth in line with local wishes and capacities.

Bibliography

K. Allen: *Growth centres and growth centre policy* in European Free Trade Association. *Regional policy in EFTA.* (Edinburgh, 1968)

K. Allen: *The regional multiplier* in S.C. Orr and J.B. Cullingworth (eds): *Regional and urban studies* (London, 1969)

G.C. Archibald: *Regional multiplier effects in the U.K.,* in *Oxford Economic Papers* (1967)

R. Artle: *The structure of the Stockholm economy* (New York, 1965)

S. Ash: *The U.K. primary aluminium industry: a case study in non-tariff barriers* (London, 1972)

Association of Scientific Workers   *Highland Power* (London, 1945)

H. Aujac: *La hierarchie des industries dans un tableau des echanges interindustriels, Revue economique,* vol. 11, March 1960

P. Aydalot: *Note sur les economies externes et quelques notions connexes, Revue economique,* vol. 16, November 1965

T. Barna: *The interdependence of the British economy* in *Journal of the Royal Statistical Society,* vol. CVX, part 1 (1952)

B.J.L. Berry and A. Pred: *Central place studies* (Philadelphia, 1965)

C Blake and S. McDowall: *A local input-output table* in *Scottish Journal of Political Economy,* vol. 14 (1967)

J. R. Boudeville: *Problems of regional economic planning* (Edinburgh, 1966)

P.J. Bourque: *An input-output analysis of economic change in Washington state* in *University of Washington Business Review* (1971)

A.J. Brown: *The Framework of Regional Economics in the United Kingdom* (Cambridge, 1972) chapter 8.

A.J. Brown et al: *The Green Paper on Development Areas in National Institute Economic Review* (1967)

S. Brubaker: *Trends in the world aluminium industry* (Baltimore, 1967)

G. Cassel: *Theoretische Sozial-Okonomie* (Leipzig, 1927)

Central Statistical Office:	*Input-output tables for the United Kingdom, 1968* (London, 1973)
H.B. Chenery and P.G. Clark:	*Interindustry economics* (New York, 1959)
W. Christaller:	*Central places in southern Germany* (Englewood Cliffs, 1965) The original German edition was published in 1933.
Y. Comay:	*Determinants of return migration: Canadian professionals in the United States* in *Southern Economic Journal* (1971)
Commission on Industrial Relations, Report No. 29:	*Alcan Smelter site* (London, 1972)
A. Currie and associates:	*The objectives of Highland development: an Easter Ross case study* (Lamington, 1973)
S. Czamanski:	*Regional science techniques in practice* (Lexington, 1972)
L.E. Davin:	*Economic regionale et croissance* (Paris, 1964)
Department of Industry:	*Input-output tables for the United Kingdom, 1970 and 1971* (London, 1974 and 1975)
S.N. Eisenstadt:	*The absorption of emigrants* (London, 1954)
European Economic Community:	*Study for the promotion of an industrial development pole in southern Italy* (Brussels, 1966)
J. Friedmann:	*Regional development policy: a case study of Venezuela* (Cambridge, Mass., 1966)
M. Gray:	*The Highland economy, 1750-1850* (Edinburgh, 1957)
M.A. Greig:	*The economic impact of the H.I.D.B. investment in fisheries* (Inverness, 1972)
M.A. Greig:	*The regional income and employment effects of a paper mill* in *Scottish Journal of Political Economy* (1971)
T. Hagerstrand:	*Aspects of the spatial structure of social communication and the diffusion of information, Papers and Proceedings of the Regional Science Association* (1966)
T. Hagerstrand:	*The propagation of innovation waves* (Lund, 1972)
M. Hagood:	*An examination of the use of factor analysis in the problem of subregional delineation* in *Rural Sociology* (1942)
N.M. Hansen:	*French regional planning* (Bloomington, 1968)

N.M. Hansen: *Intermediate-size cities as growth centres* (New York, 1971)

T. Hermansen: *Development poles and development centres in national and regional development in* A.R. Kuklinski (ed): *Growth poles and growth centres in national and regional planning* (The Hague, 1972)

G.J.D. Hewings: *Regional input-output models in the U.K.* in *Regional Studies,* vol. 5 (1971)

H.I.D.B: *First Report* (Inverness, 1967)

W.Z. Hirsch: *Interindustry relations of a metropolitan area* in *Review of Economics and Statistics,* vol. XLI, November 1959

A.O. Hirschman: *The strategy of economic development* (New Haven, 1958)

W. Isard: *Methods of regional analysis* (Cambridge, Mass., 1960)

L. H. Klaassen: *Area economic and social redevelopment* (Paris, 1965)

A.R. Kuklinski (ed):   *Growth poles and growth centres in national and regional planning* (The Hague, 1972)

Labour Party: *Report of the 66th Annual Conference of the Labour Party, Scarborough, 1967* (London, 1967)

W. Leontief: *Quantitative input-output relations in the economic system of the United States* in *The Review of Economics and Statistics,* vol. XVIII (August, 1936)

A. Losch: *The economics of location* (New Haven, 1954) The original German edition was published in 1940.

G.A. Mackay: *Prospects for the Moray Firth sub-region* (Aberdeen, 1975)

I.H. McNicoll: *The Shetland economy* (Glasgow, 1976)

G. Manners: *Misplacing the smelters* in *New Society,* 16th May, 1968

W.H. Miernyk: *Impact of the space program on a local economy* (Morgantown, 1967)

E. Miller: *Return and non-return inmigration* in *Growth and change* (1973)

F.T. Moore and J.W. Petersen: *Regional analysis: an interindustry model of Utah* in *Review of Economics and Statistics,* vol. XXVII, November, 1955

W.I. Morrison:	*The development of an urban interindustry model,* three articles in each of parts 3 to 5 of *Environment and Planning,* vol. 5, (1973)
G. Myrdal:	*Economic theory and underdeveloped regions* (London, 1957)
E. Nevin, A.R. Roe and J.I. Round	*The structure of the Welsh economy* (Cardiff, 1966)
P.C. Newman:	*The development of economic thought* (Englewood Cliffs, 1952)
P.Nijkamp:	*Planning of industrial complexes* (Rotterdam, 1972)
North of Scotland College of Agriculture:	*An agro-economic appraisal of agriculture in Easter Ross* (Aberdeen, 1967)
J.Ormiston:	*Moray Firth: An agricultural study* (Inverness, 1973)
S.C. Orr and J.B. Cullingworth (eds):	*Regional and urban studies* (London, 1969)
J. Paelinck:	*La theorie du developpement regionale polarise, Cahiers de l'I.S.E.A., L.15 (1965)*
J.B. Parr:	*Growth poles, regional development and central place theory, Papers of the Regional Science Association,* vol. 31 (1973)
F. Perroux:	*Economic space: theory and applications,* in *Quarterly Journal of Economics,* vol. 64, No. 1, February 1950
F. Perroux:	*"Note sur la notion de pole de croissance," Economic applique,* nos. 1-2, January-June 1955
E. Richards:	*The leviathan of wealth* (London, 1973)
H.W. Richardson:	*Growth pole spillovers: the dynamics of backwash and spread, Regional studies,* vol. 10, no. 1 (1976)
F. Rosenfeld:	*Les firmes motrices et la comptabilite regionale, Cahiers de l'I.S.E.A., L.11 (1962)*
P. Sadler, B. Archer and C. Owen:	*Regional income multipliers* (Bangor, 1973)
J.A. Schumpeter:	*"The theory of economic development"* (New York, 1954) The original German edition was published in 1912.
G.P.F. Steed:	*Commodity flows and interindustry linkages of Northern Ireland's manufacturing industries*

D.B. Steele:	*Regional multipliers in Great Britain* in *Oxford Economic Papers* (1969)
I.G. Stewart:	*Input-output table for the United Kingdom* in *The London and Cambridge Economic Bulletin, The Times Review of Industry,* (December, 1958)
W. Thompson:	*A preface to urban economics* (Baltimore, 1965)
J.E. Tilton:	*International diffusion of technology: the case of the semi-conductors* (New York, 1971)
J. Vanderkamp:	*Interregional mobility in Canada: a study of the time pattern of migration* in *Canadian Journal of Economics* (1968)
J.J. Van Duijn:	*An interregional model of economic fluctuations* (Farnborough, 1972)
T. Wilson:	*The regional multiplier: a critique* in *Oxford Economic Papers* (1968)